How to Start a Professional Organizing Business

Enjoy the Fruitfulness of Working for Yourself by Establishing a Clutter-Free Home for Your Clients

Everleigh Maldonado

© **Copyright 2024 - All rights reserved.**

The content contained within this book may not be reproduced, duplicated or transmitted without direct written permission from the author or the publisher.

Under no circumstances will any blame or legal responsibility be held against the publisher, or author, for any damages, reparation, or monetary loss due to the information contained within this book, either directly or indirectly.

Legal Notice:

This book is copyright protected. It is only for personal use. You cannot amend, distribute, sell, use, quote or paraphrase any part, or the content within this book, without the consent of the author or publisher.

Disclaimer Notice:

Please note the information contained within this document is for educational and entertainment purposes only. All effort has been executed to present accurate, up to date, reliable, complete information. No warranties of any kind are declared or implied. Readers acknowledge that the author is not engaging in the rendering of legal, financial, medical or professional advice. The content within this book has been derived from various sources.

Please consult a licensed professional before attempting any techniques outlined in this book.

By reading this document, the reader agrees that under no circumstances is the author responsible for any losses, direct or indirect, that are incurred as a result of the use of information contained within this document, including, but not limited to, errors, omissions, or inaccuracies.

Table of Contents

Introduction..5

Chapter 1: Establishing Your Organizing Business...6

Chapter 2: Determining Your Niche, Answering What Do You Do, and Creating a Plan............38

Chapter 3: Tips When You're Organizing Spaces..59

Chapter 4: How to Determine Your Rates as a Professional Organizer...........................78

Chapter 5: Considerations for Your Agreement Form...91

Chapter 6: How to Have a Successful Initial Consultation with Your Clients....................102

Chapter 7: How Do You Get Clients as a Professional Organizer...........................121

Conclusion..143

Introduction

Starting your own business is exciting no doubt! My guess is that you're reading this book because you love all things organizing and for one reason or another you're thinking that starting your own professional organizing business is a great idea! Well, let me tell you that I would have to agree with your line of thinking. However, starting a business is not all sunshine and rainbows. There is a lot of serious upfront work that you must put into your business just to get it started. Then there's all of the work you have to do to gain your first set of customers, and now the real work can begin where you can finally get your hands moving and start organizing. Not to worry though, this book is going to help guide you through the things you need to do to be successful in this industry.

Chapter 1: Establishing Your Organizing Business

Before you can just jump straight into organizing other people's homes, there's some groundwork that we need to take care of first. If you're anything like me when I was first starting out, then you're probably unsure of where exactly it is that you need to begin. So before I start to cover some of the things that you need to think about, I want to share with you where I was before I started this business. Before I became a professional organizer, I had never run my own business or done anything entrepreneurial for that matter. I graduated from college and found myself working at a nonprofit. The pay was okay and the work was fulfilling but I found myself getting burnt out a lot. As time went on I started a family and as my family grew, I decided I'd rather be a stay-at-home parent than work just to pay for daycare and insurance. However, as my kids started to enter school, I found myself wanting to do something more with my time. I wanted to reignite the passion that I had felt at times when I was in the non-profit world. The difference was I wanted to do things my way. I didn't want to deal with all of the work politics, late nights, and having to feel like you're begging just to get a day off. So I started to look at my passions first and see if I could do something related to that. Fortunately, I stumbled across the idea of being a professional organizer, which seemed wild to me when I first heard about it. As it turns out, I really did like staying organized because I had to in an effort to keep my sanity as a mother of 3. So I figured why not dive in and start a business around this? The thing is you shouldn't just dive in and get your first customer. There are some steps you need to take before you get your first paying client. So my first piece of advice to you is to be patient. This applies not only to the start of your business, but throughout the entirety of your entrepreneurial journey. You have to be patient to lay the foundation so you're ready for your first client. But there are going to be plenty of other times when you're going to need to be patient for various different reasons. It could be that you're not gaining clients as fast as you'd like. Your social media posts could be getting less engagement than you would like. You could have a record-breaking month and then the next month is mediocre. A business is very different from a 9-5 job. With a job you know how much you're getting paid and it's going to stay the same regardless of how much income the company you work for is generating. As a business owner, this is not the case and your income can fluctuate rapidly. Of course, if you spend any amount of time on social media trying to learn about business, you will never hear about fluctuations. It's always about how someone is making 6 figures or how they made 10k within their first 90 days. Stories like this can certainly be inspiring, but they can also make you feel down on yourself if you're not seeing the same level of success. The customers, the social media likes, it will all come in due time if you're patient. There are a lot of psychological battles you'll face though that you simply won't know about until you're in it. So I'm here to let you know that it's okay. You don't have to worry if you started your business 3 months ago and haven't had your first paying client yet. I say so what? As long as you're making progress, it will come. Everyone has their own circumstances and their own pace. So it may very well be the case that you only have 5 hours a week to work on your business. It could take you 3 months just to get everything set up. This is why you shouldn't compare yourself to other people you see online. They're dealing with totally different circumstances from you. So stay patient, focus on yourself, and strive for improvement. If you do these things, then you have no reason to be upset with yourself. Now with that being the case, here are the things you'll need to think about to get the foundation laid for your business before you take on your first paying customer.

Wait, Isn't Money What Matters Most in Business?

There are two different schools of thought when it comes to starting a business. The first group of people believe that you should just start by trying to generate revenue for your business as soon as possible. The other things can be set up later, but you need to focus on revenue immediately. The other line of thinking is that you should get things set up first before you try and land your first paying customer. Sure each school of thought has its own merit, and yes I do believe that generating revenue is the most important aspect of business. However, once you take on paying clients, it becomes that much harder to have the time to set things up properly. This can lead to certain things never getting done at all, or possibly being done worse than they could have been. It puts you in scramble mode to get your business set up all the while trying to juggle your customers. It simply doesn't have to be that way. It's easier to just slow down and do things the proper way the first time around. Yes, this means it's likely going to be a few weeks or possibly months before you create your first dollar in revenue, but at least you'll feel good about pressing forward. I mean this is an organizing business at the end of the day, so doesn't it make sense that your business itself is organized?

Coming Up with a Business Name

The first thing you'll want to do as part of this process is come up with a business name. This is an important thing to do as I would recommend that you register your business. With that being the case, it's important to carefully consider the name you'd like to use. This isn't something you just want to come up with off the top of your head and immediately go with it. Who knows, you might wake up the next day and not like the name as much as you initially did. So here are some pointers when it comes to a business name and how you should approach things:

Come Up With Something that is Easy to Remember

Mistake number one when it comes to a business name is creating a name that's difficult to remember or hard to spell. Why is this a problem? Well, imagine someone tries to conduct an online search to lookup your website, but they're having trouble getting the spelling right and now your business isn't coming up. It also makes things harder for word of mouth to happen if people can't remember the name of your business. Let's pretend that you were running a farm where you have apple, peach, and orange trees. You decide to name your farm business Sherry's Very Happy and Cherry Applez Farm to have a fun play on words. Well, this name would be bad for a couple of reasons, even though it sounds playful. The first reason is that the name is too long. It's going to make things difficult for people to remember. Sure you can easily remember the name of your business and the words themselves don't seem complicated enough, but you have to remember that this is your business. People on the outside are viewing it from a totally different lens because they don't have the same attachment to it. Secondly, having a unique spelling of the word apple by having a z instead of an s is a problem as well. This is going to make it challenging when someone does an online search for your business. Imagine a friend tells their colleague about your business in person and when the colleague searches online for you, they're going to spell the word apples with an s and not a z, which hurts your chances of coming up. Thirdly, long business names create issues for your domain. Are you really going to have that long of a domain name? You probably aren't, which means your domain will be a shorter version of your business name. Again this can create the possibility of confusion. And lastly, there's one more reason why a name like the one in this example would be a dud:

Your Business Name Needs to Clearly Convey What You Do

With the example of this tree farm, the name itself creates confusion. Do you only sell apples? Do you sell cherries as well? It's hard to tell from the name itself. You might think it's no big deal because you can clear up any potential questions that a customer might have. What if you never had the chance to do so? What if someone is looking for peaches, and based on your name they assume that you don't sell peaches so they move on to someone else? Something like this happens more than you think. Have you ever watched a commercial and at the end of it wondered what product was trying to be sold to you or who the company was that was trying to sell the product? I know that I sure have. So using a word like organizing, tidying, or similar synonyms makes sense to help make it obvious as to what you do. That is important. You want things to be simple and obvious to someone who has never heard of your business before.

Create a List of Names

Yes, it is possible that you can come up with a home run name right off the bat. It's more likely though that if you give yourself a few days, you can come up with something even better. Again, this is the advantage of taking things a bit slower to ensure that everything is done right. Sure, you can rush through things to get to your first client as soon as possible, but that's how you end up with a name that you end up hating as time goes on. Instead, give yourself a few days and come up with a list of names. Ideally, you'd want to come up with a list of 10-15 different name ideas. If you're struggling to come up with ideas, then don't worry because you have the internet on your side. You can use a website such as Fiverr and pay someone to come up with name ideas for your business. If you want some free options, then you can post on an online forum asking for ideas or ask in organizing Facebook Groups for some suggestions. Once you have your list of names ready to go, you're not done yet.

Ask for Your Friend's Opinions on the Names

Even if you have a name idea that you like, you're not done yet. This is true even if the name checks all of the boxes in your eyes. Just because something makes sense in your head does not mean that it will make sense to other people. This is why it's a good idea to take your name suggestions and ask your friends and family which of the names they like the best. The key is to then ask them why they chose the name that they did. Ask them if the name makes it obvious as to what kind of business this is. I would get at least 10 different opinions on your name ideas. You could even take to the internet and have people vote as well. You don't have to go with the name idea that got the most votes, but that is a good indication of which direction you should look towards.

Ultimately though, it's your business so the choice is yours. If there's a name you really want to go with and hope that people choose, you can ask them why they didn't pick a certain name. This can help to give you insights into how you should possibly tweak that name to make it resonate more with your customer base.

Sleep on It

Once you have a name that you've decided you want to move forward with, take at least one night and sleep on it. See if the name still resonates with you like it did when you first came up with the idea. If it does, then great you can move forward with things. If not, then you may need to go back to the drawing board. Your business name should be something that you like and enjoy as long as it checks all of the boxes and makes sense to your customers.

Checking for Availability

Now that you have a name that fits the necessary criteria and is something you like, you can move to the next step, which is to check and make sure the name you want is available to use. There are a few things you're going to want to check to make sure you're good to go. The first is making sure the business name is available to be used in your state. You can conduct a search on your Secretary of State's website, or you can use a company to run the search for you. If the name isn't available to be used in your state, you're going to need to come up with something else. With everything else, there are potential workarounds if you really like the name. You're going to run into a dead end though if there's already a different business using the name you'd like to go with. If it passes though and the name is available for use in your state, then you can move your search to the next phase, which is going to be domain name availability. You can check for domain name availability using something like Squarespace. The type of domain name that you want to be available is the .com version of your domain name. If that isn't available, then you have a few options. The first is to use .org, .net, or something else along those lines. This of course does not look as professional as having a .com domain name. The other option you have is to come up with a slightly different version of your business name so that you can have .com availability. You can do this by adding in an additional word to your business name or changing things up a bit. So if your business name was Sherry's Organizing Business and that domain name wasn't available, then you could use a domain name such as sherryorganizes.com or sherrysprofessionalorganizingbusiness.com. The problem is that using a .net or changing things up for your domain name is less than ideal. If you have to change up your business name in order to get a .com domain name, then you run the risk of creating customer confusion. This will make it harder for people to find you when they're searching online. You'll tell people that your business name is Sherry's Organizing Business, but you might not come up in search results if your domain name is too different from that. Or you'll have to tell people that your business name is Sherry's Organizing Business but your website name is SherryGetsYouOrganizied.com. That will definitely confuse people and it will hurt word of mouth and people being able to find you online. This is why it's better to have a name that has availability for everything that you need it for. Sure you can do a workaround like I've just mentioned, but that's far from ideal. The last thing you're going to want to do a check on is social media handles. For every platform that you potentially think you want to be on, go ahead and check and see if there's availability on the platform for the name that you want to use. If the name isn't open on every platform, that might not be the end of the world. If you primarily plan on using two different platforms, then those 2 would be the most important to make sure that the handle would be available for you to use. If everything checks out, then you'll want to go ahead and snag up the social media handle names and the website domain name, and then you can begin the process of establishing your business so that you can secure the name for usage in your state. The reason why you'll want to do things in this order is because you're going from easiest to hardest. You can easily snag social media handles and a domain name fairly easily as well. The process of registering your business with the state you reside in can take a bit of time. So what you don't want to happen is you wait on your social media handle names until your business is officially formed and then in the meantime someone snags the domain name right out from under you. It's free to create your social media accounts and securing a domain name is really cheap as well, typically only costing in the realm of $20 per year to maintain, so you might as well do it as soon as you can!

Creating Your Business Entity

Now it's time to actually form your business. Before you do that though, you must decide on what kind of entity you want your business to be. The first type of entity is a C corporation. Under this classification, you can have an unlimited number of shareholders and it's the most common entity for big businesses. If your plan is to grow a large corporation, then this would likely be your most ideal choice. However, my guess is that for most people reading this book, a C corporation is not going to make the most sense. An S corporation is different from a C corporation in terms of how it is taxed, and you are limited to 100 shareholders or less among other things. After this, you essentially have two remaining options with those being a sole proprietorship and a Limited Liability Company or LLC for short. The main difference between the two boils down to asset protection. If you have personal assets that you want to protect, then an LLC is a good option for you to look into. As far as tax purposes are concerned, the IRS views an LLC as a disregarded entity. This means that an LLC is taxed as a sole proprietorship. If you're a single-member LLC, then you can file a Schedule C with your personal taxes. If you're a limited partnership, then you'll file a separate federal return and each member will receive Form 1065 that can be used when filing their personal returns. However, if you don't want your LLC to be taxed as a sole proprietorship, then you can elect to be taxed as an S corporation. Doing this is a good idea as you start to generate a significant amount of income as this will help to save you money on your taxes. If you are creating this business with someone else, then you'll want to form a partnership or a limited partnership. When it comes to forming a business by yourself or with another person, you really need to think about the decision carefully. If you form a partnership, then it's not just about you, it's about you and another person. The profit is going to be shared, so you really need to carefully consider the type of person you'd form a partnership with. When it comes to forming a partnership, you ideally would want the person to have strengths that cover up your weaknesses and vice versa. So let's say you're really sound on the organizing side of things, but you're not so strong when it comes to marketing and sales. Your ideal type of business partner would be someone who is strong in those areas. This would allow your business partner to focus on generating leads while you can focus on fulfilling the service to the clients. Ideally, with a partnership, the idea is that the two of you can generate more revenue than either of you would be able to do on your own. Even if you have someone in mind who has strengths that you don't, you need to think about the person's work ethic and how you like working with the person. If your personality and their personality don't mesh well, then you are going to resent your business over time. If the other person is only working 10 hours a week in the business and you're working 60 hours a week, then you're going to resent your partner. This is why you have to consider multiple angles when it comes to picking the right person. Picking a friend whom you already know can be a good thing or a bad thing. You can't pick someone solely because you know who they are. Forming a partnership with someone you know can work well if you know the personalities are a fit and you know they have a strong work ethic. Sometimes though friends can be lazy because they don't feel accountable to their friends like they would with a boss from a typical job. You might not even be considering a partnership, but if you are, these are some points you'll want to take some time and ponder over. No matter which entity type you are thinking about, it's best to consult with a professional to get guidance for the entity type that is best for your situation. For myself, I like the idea of having asset protection and an LLC is an easy choice for me. I used a company called Bizee to help form my LLC and there are plenty of other good companies out there that provide a similar service, such as Legal Zoom. The thing I really liked about using another company to help me form my business was that it took the guesswork out of the equation for me. You might not be sure where to start either, so it's worth looking into a service like this if it's your first time forming a company.

Another Difference with an LLC

There is another difference that exists between a sole proprietorship and an LLC. With an LLC, you'll need to appoint a registered agent for your business. The registered agent is someone who receives legal documents on your behalf. You can appoint yourself to be your own registered agent. However, you can appoint a separate company to be your registered agent and the service is not that much, it's usually only $100-$200 per year depending on who you go with. If you form your business through a company like Bizee, this is a service you can add on. What are the benefits of doing this? Well, this prevents your home address or the address your business is operating from being on the public record where anyone would have access. In the case of a professional organizing business, it is likely going to be the case that you're going to be operating from your own home, so this is an important consideration. Even if you are renting an office space, it's still a good idea to have a registered agent that's someone other than yourself. This will help to dramatically cut back on the amount of junk mail that you'll start to receive once you start your business. Credit card offers, office supplies, companies saying you need to buy a poster to be compliant, the list goes on and on. Sure having a separate registered agent won't totally prevent these things, but it will help to reduce them greatly.

Business Bank Account

Another important consideration you're going to need to think about is a business bank account. No matter which entity type you move forward with, having a separate bank account for your business finances is a good idea. You might think that it's easier if you keep everything together in one place with your personal finances, but this is far from the case. Soon enough, things will start to become a mess. From a bookkeeping perspective, you're constantly going to be sorting through all of your personal transactions and separating them from your business transactions. It's easier to log into a separate account and see only your business transactions. If you decide to operate your business as an LLC for example, then this will help to make your business look like an actual business instead of you looking like you're running a sole proprietorship. The good news is that you can easily set up a business bank account completely online if you want to. If you want to go to a bank in person and set one up that way, you can do that as well. Some good online options that I recommend are Novo, Bluevine, and Lili, but there are plenty of other good ones out there. You'll want to look at the features each bank can offer you and see what matters most to you. Some will allow you to transfer more money per month than others. Some will let you open up sub-accounts under your main account. This is really handy as it can allow you to keep a separate account for savings and taxes among other things. Some banks have better interest rates than others. So it really all boils down to your preferences when it comes to banking, but no matter what be sure to create a new account that will strictly deal with your business income and expenses.

Set Aside Money for Taxes

Speaking of taxes, something else you're going to need to think about is setting aside money for taxes. When you work for someone else as an employee, money is automatically withheld from your paycheck. So when you're working for someone else, you don't have to think about taxes too much throughout the year. Things change though when you're running your own business. None of your income is going to be withheld for taxes. It's all on you to ensure that you're setting aside some of your income for taxes. This is where it can make things a little complicated if all of your finances are in one account. I like having the option of a separate subaccount so that way I can move some money into the other account and not have to worry about it. Then when it comes time to pay taxes, the money that I need is there. What you don't want to do is treat all of the income that you get as your own, spend it, and then not have any money when your taxes are due. It's an easy mistake that a lot of new entrepreneurs make because they're used to getting paychecks where they can freely spend the money that was deposited into their account. Depending on what your business income is will determine if you'll have to pay quarterly taxes or not. Typically if your business is expected to owe more than $1,000 in taxes for the year, you will be expected to pay quarterly taxes, but this can vary depending on your business entity. Quarterly taxes are typically due around the midpoint of April, June, September, and January. You can make your estimated tax payments on the official IRS website. It is best to consult with a professional CPA when you start your business to ensure you are squared away with your taxes when it comes to your given entity type.

Bookkeeping

Another thing you'll want to keep track of is your business transactions. Another difference between being your own boss and being an employee is that you can deduct business expenses. This means that you're only being taxed on the profit that your business generated and not the total amount of revenue. Let's say you generated a total of $80,000, but your business expenses totaled $15,000 for the year. Your business profit came out to be

$65,000 and this is the number you will be taxed on. This means that it's really important to keep track of your expenses so that you can deduct expenses that are being used to help grow your business. For example, let's say that you go out and spend $100 on social media ads. This is an expense that you have because you're trying to grow your business. If your business did not exist, then you would not have this expense. So you can deduct that $100 from your total revenue to help lessen your tax bill. Anything has the potential to be a tax deduction so long as it is necessary for your business. So for example, if you were running a daycare, then buying diapers would be a necessary expense. However, if you were opening a hair salon and you bought diapers and tried to claim them as a tax deduction, then that wouldn't make sense and could raise a red flag. You can do your own bookkeeping using something like a spreadsheet, or you can hire a professional. There are plenty of great tutorials online about how you can be your own bookkeeper using a spreadsheet, and this isn't a bad option to consider when you're starting out as this will be the easiest time to be your own bookkeeper. However, you might not want to mess with it and would rather have someone else handle this for you so that you can focus on the many other things necessary to grow your business.

Business Insurance

As a professional organizer, you might think that there's not much risk when it comes to this profession. I would have to agree with you that there are plenty of other businesses out there that are far more dangerous than this one. Even if that is the case, it's still a good idea to protect yourself. There are numerous things that could happen even if they aren't that likely to occur. You might donate something that the client didn't want you to. Someone might get hurt tripping over the clutter that's in the house, or trip over a pile of items that you created. The client might claim that you stole something from their home. There are plenty of possibilities that you need to be prepared for. The most common forms of insurance that you'll likely need are going to be general liability and errors and omission insurance, but be sure to work with a professional insurance agent who can help provide you with the best coverage that will suit your specific business needs.

Build Your Website

Another key aspect of getting your business going is creating your website. As part of the first steps in the process, you would have already checked for domain name availability and bought your domain name. This is a great start, but now you'll want to go ahead and fully flesh out your website. A website is like your digital business card in the modern age. A business not having a website is kind of like not having a cell phone, it just doesn't make sense to not have one. Your website will act as a constant advertisement for your business and it will make you visible to your potential customers. So it's important to get something up as soon as you can. Before I get into the finer details of how to go about building your website and what it should contain, I first want to share with you the mentality you should have about your website. Your website is never complete and it's always a work in progress. When you think of things in this manner, you're not going to delay sharing your website with the world. Instead, it will be sufficient, look as good as it can, and you'll publish it to the world. As time goes on, you can improve upon things. So with that being said, what are your options when it comes to creating your website? Really it's going to boil down to you doing things yourself or hiring someone else to create your website for you. A DIY option may sound scary to you, but it actually isn't. This is due to the fact that there are plenty of platforms out there that offer simple drag-and-drop templates to make creating your website a simple process. There is also a wide range of tutorials online that you can follow along with. You can use a platform like Squarespace, Wix, or Wordpress to create your own website. The other option is to hire a company or freelancer to create things the way you want. Depending on who you hire, this will easily cost in the hundreds or thousands of dollars. The benefit to this is that you won't have to worry about things not looking exactly the way you want or struggling to get something to work or look right. What I recommend you do if you're unsure is watch a tutorial online and get a feel for the process, and see if it's something you think you'd be interested in doing. If it isn't, then look to hire someone. You might not have the budget to be able to hire someone, and in that case, you're going to have to do it yourself, but keep in mind you can always hire someone to complete a small task as needed and this will be much cheaper than hiring someone to make a website from scratch. For example, let's say you're struggling to get some text to left align on your website. You could hire a freelancer on Fiverr or Upwork to fix this one specific issue. Paying for this and other small pain points that you might encounter along the way will help to save you money. You'll also want to ensure that your website is mobile responsive. This means that your website will be adjusted and will look different when someone is on your website from their mobile device as opposed to their desktop. Many of the templates that you'll use to build out your website will be mobile responsive, you'll just want to make sure of this before you get too far into the process. If you create your entire website only to realize it's not mobile responsive, you can hire a web developer to help make your website mobile responsive. This is an absolute must in today's world where everyone has a phone. People aren't going to spend their time trying to navigate through small text and scrolling side to side to get the information they're looking for. Instead, they're just going to quickly leave and never come back.

Website Basics

When it comes to building your website, sure you have the domain name, but this isn't the only thing that you need. You also need a website host. Think of the domain name like a home address. Imagine though that you go to a friend's address for a visit but they're not home. What good does that do you? This is where the website host comes into play. The website host ensures that someone is home 24/7 so to speak. In website terminology, this means your website is available for people to visit at all times. If you have a domain name without a host, nothing will come up when people go to that address. The cost of a website host will vary. It could cost you as little as $10-$20 per month or you could pay upwards of $30-$50 or more per month depending on which company you choose to go with and what package you choose. One big determining factor for the price of your host is going to come down to the amount of traffic that your website receives on a monthly basis. Website traffic is simply the number of visitors that your website has. The more people that visit your website, the more strain it's going to be on the servers of the company that's hosting your website. This is where things like website speed or your website potentially crashing can be an issue. Luckily though that isn't something you likely have to worry about right now. You can start with a basic package and as your website traffic starts to increase, you can then consider upgrading to accommodate for the additional visitors. You can get your website hosted through the same company that you build your website through such as Wix, Squarespace, or WP Engine in the case of Wordpress, or you can go with a different host provider such as Hostinger or Dreamhost.

What Pages Should Your Website Contain?

If you go to just about any website, most of them will have a basic setup. There of course is the homepage, which is the first page that people will land on when they visit the basic domain name of your website. Aside from that, your website should also include an about me section, a contact page, a page where you can post any blog articles that you want to post, and a page where people can book a consultation with you. If your website has these things, then it will be able to do its job. So in your case, what is the purpose of your website? It's for people to learn more information about you and your business to help warm them up and ultimately help guide them into booking a consultation with you. So your about me page is designed for people to learn more about you. People don't want to work with strangers. They want to know more about the person they are working with, and this isn't strictly in a professional sense. So if you like riding horses or traveling, mention that. You'll want to talk about what you enjoy doing in your spare time as well as how it is you got into the business of organizing. For your blog articles, you'll want to post helpful tips and information to help people get and stay organized. There really is no limit to how long or short your articles need to be and you can post as frequently as you like, but I do recommend posting at least once per week. If you go months at a time without posting to your blog, then it makes your website seem dead like you haven't cared about it for months. Your contact me page is a very simple page where someone will enter their email and then there will be a text box where they can ask their question. This is a great way to capture leads of people who are potentially interested in hiring you. And of course, you'll want to have a page where people can book an initial consultation with you. Different people will be at different stages in the buying process. Some people will want to learn more about you, which is where the about me and blog articles will come into play. Some people though will be ready to take action now. So without this page, you will be missing out on sales that's for sure.

Google My Business

Once you have your website set up, it's now time to create a Google My Business account. What this will do is allow your business to appear in search results. So for example, when you go online and you type in dry cleaners near me, a list of various different dry cleaners in your area are going to pop up. You can look at each individual business and see their online reviews, look at their website, and compare them to other dry cleaners so you can make an informed decision. You want to do the same thing for your business. When people search online for something like "professional organizer near me" or "organizer in New Orleans" you'll want your business to come up in the search results. Initially, your business isn't going to have any reviews, and depending on what the competition is like in your area, your rankings might not be that good. That's totally reasonable though since you just started. So be patient with yourself and as time goes on, you will build up your reviews and rise through the ranks. Even though you're starting from nothing, this is still an important step that you'll want to take.

Google Workspace

The next thing you'll want to do is use Google Workspace to help create your business email address. You can only do this once you've purchased your domain name, so make sure that's taken care of first. Through Google Workspace, you can create your own professional email address. So if you've ever seen an email address such as support@chadscustomcomputers.com or something along those lines, this is one way that you can go about doing so. Having an email address like this creates a very professional look for your business. Think about any large-sized corporation that you know of. All of their email addresses are at their own domain name, and yours should be as well, especially considering that it isn't that expensive. It only costs around $5 per month to create a professional email like this. Since you're likely going to be starting off this business by yourself, you don't need a support email and one with your name in it, just create one email with your name in it such as sherry@sherrygetsyouorganized.com for example.

Chapter 2: Determining Your Niche, Answering What Do You Do, and Creating a Plan

If you've made it to this point, then go ahead and pat yourself on the back. You've done a lot of work to get to this point to lay the groundwork for your business. I know you're eager to start serving your first client, but there are still some things that you need to think about first before you start working with paying clients. The things that I'm about to go over in this chapter are things that most people never think about. They just try to dive right in and then they'll wonder why they aren't seeing the success that they want to. A little bit of patience and planning can go a long way in business. And that's what this chapter is all about, so let's kick things off by talking about your niche.

What is a Niche and Why Does it Matter?

A niche is a subtopic of a category. You can think of a niche in a macro or micro sense. If you were thinking of a niche in a macro sense you could say that you're in the organizing business compared to the food industry, retail, or any of the other numerous fields out there.

You can also think of a niche in the micro sense such as a niche within the organization field. So in this case, this is what we want to think about. What niche within the organizing business do you want to specialize in? But wait, you might be thinking why do I even need to specialize in a niche? Why not just take on any client that wants to work with me? Yes, on the surface this makes sense. I'm not saying if someone reaches out to you that you should deny them because they aren't in your target niche. What I am saying is your niche will give you guidance on how you market your company and this will in turn determine who you attract and ultimately who you work with. Still, though, why does that matter? Why not just try to appeal to anyone you can? Here are some reasons why having a niche is a good idea:

It's More Fun

By selecting a niche, you get to work with the type of person that you actually want to work with. For example, maybe your niche is working with clients after they've experienced a loss in their life. You resonate with this niche because you've experienced loss in your own life in this example. Wouldn't this clientele mean more to you and wouldn't you enjoy working with them more as opposed to someone else? You're going to be working really hard to make your business successful, so you might as well work with people that you are going to get the most fulfillment out of.

You'll Work with Better Clients

Not only will you be working with people that you enjoy more, but they'll tend to be better clients. Of course, there's no way that you can totally prevent working with someone who's a bit extra, but your niche can ensure that you're not attracting the wrong type of client. For example, maybe you don't want to work with hoarders. They have a hard time letting go of things and this is a journey you don't like walking down with people. By specializing in something else, you can help to bring in a different clientele from the type of person that you don't want to work with.

There Are Plenty of Fish Out There

The reality is that even with picking a niche, there are plenty of people out there who will fit in your category, which means there's still a pool of people that you can market to who will be interested in your business. So don't worry about if the niche is too small and instead focus more on what will give you the most joy and fulfillment. The larger a niche is, the more people it will contain, but that means there will also be more competition. The opposite is true the smaller a niche is. Either way, there are plenty of people to go around who will be in need of your service, so don't worry about not having enough people to market to.

Gives Your Marketing Efforts a Sense of Direction

This is a big one. What having a niche will do for you is you will be able to clearly speak to a select group of people when you are creating content and doing other such promotions for your business. There is no shortage of advertisements and social media content out there. So if you're throwing food against the wall and hoping that something will stick, you are going to be saddened by your results. By creating content without a niche in mind, you're going to get lost in the vast sea with everything else that's going on. No one will pay much attention to you and you'll be left wondering why you're failing. The main reason is because your content isn't resonating with anyone, and how can it when you're not creating your content and other promotional material through the lens of a specific niche? Imagine a post that speaks in generic terms vs one that speaks through the lens of someone who has recently lost a loved one. Which type of post do you think is going to resonate more with someone who has lost a loved one? Obviously, it's going to be the post that's more specific. Again the fear here is that you won't be appealing to anyone who hasn't experienced a tough loss. But remember what I just talked about, there are plenty of fish out there. As sad as it is, death is a part of life, and there are plenty of people out there who have experienced a loss in their life, which means there are more than enough people who will resonate with your material. Since you are making your content with one person in mind, whenever that type of person sees your marketing materials, they're going to be that much more likely to respond to it, which is the whole point of marketing in the first place. Think about this in your own life. Have you ever heard an ad and thought to yourself, "Wow that's me!" If you have, then this shows the company did a great job of resonating with their niche and you were that much more likely to purchase the product or service. That's the moment we're trying to create with your audience. We want them to think, "Wow that described my situation perfectly, I have to reach out." The only way that you can achieve this is by carefully selecting a niche and not being general.

What Are Some Niches That You Can Choose From?

There is no shortage of niches in the organization field. So you can really go with anything that you think you will enjoy, but here are some ideas to give you a place to start from:

-People who have recently moved due to divorce
-People who have experienced the loss of a loved one
-Empty nesters or their kid moving off to college
-People who are welcoming in a new child to their home
-People with ADHD or OCD
-People who struggle to let things go and tend to hoard
-People whose parents or parent are moving in with them

-Room specializations such as the kitchen, kid's bedroom, living, etc. This can even get as niched down to specific areas within a room such as a bedroom closet or pantry

This just scratches the surface of possibilities that's out there, but as you can see there are plenty of amazing niches that you could dive into. And with any one of these niches it's easy to see how much more it would speak to someone when you're really able to dive in and talk about the specific pain points that this group of people would be experiencing.

How to Pick Your Niche

An easy place to start when picking your niche is to start with something that resonated with you specifically. Maybe you have experienced a tough loss in your life, or you know it can be hard to utilize the extra space that comes after a child moves out. You could struggle to keep your pantry organized and so that holds a special place for you to help others. By choosing something that has a special meaning to you, it's going to help you put in that much more effort with your clients and it will show. You shouldn't pick something solely because you think you can make the most money from it. There's money to be made in any niche and in the long run, you'll make more when something holds special value to you. What if you're not sure what you like or what you should specialize in between two different niches? This is where you can enlist the help of your friends. Ask them which of the two niches sounds more like you and get their opinions. Your friends know you better than anyone else after all, so their opinions can help to guide you. If you need a niche in general, you can ask them what they think your speciality should be. Another way you can approach this is by asking your friends what they think your strengths are. Let's say for the sake of this example that your friends say you're really good at getting things started and following through. Well, your specialty could be helping people who struggle with your strength, such as people who struggle with procrastination.

Determining the Pain Points of Your Niche

Once you've decided on a niche, your work is not yet complete. Having a niche will give you direction and help increase your chances of landing clients, but you need to go deep to truly reap the benefits that having a niche can offer you. You need to understand the pains and frustrations of your niche so that you can more directly speak to them. This is why choosing a niche that you struggle with personally or something that resonates with you is important. If this is the case, then you'll already understand the pains, frustrations, and sorrows that can come from dealing with the problem that you are. For example, maybe you've had a parent, sibling, or in law move in with you. What were some of the pain points you experienced as part of this process? You had to clean out an extra room, and clean out the closet, where is all of the stuff from the closet going to go? These are all things that people are dealing with who are going through something similar, so you can help them by understanding them. So step one to diving deep into pain points is think of your own life and see if you can relate. What if you can't relate to your given niche? What do you do in this case? Well, you'll want to do research on people who are in that given niche. If you know of anyone who's in your niche, ask them about the pain points that they experience as it relates to the niche and staying organized. So if your niche is helping a parent get organized after their child moved out, ask them about what troubles they've been experiencing in regards to what they're doing with the extra space and how they're keeping it organized. If you don't have any friends that you can ask, you can always take to the internet. Post on groups and forums and simply state that you're doing some market research for a professional organizing company that you're starting, and then ask what issues people are experiencing when it comes to staying organized after a child has moved out or whatever your niche is. It's also a good idea to join online groups that deal with your target audience. So for instance, you would join empty nester groups on Facebook. You'd then start to scroll through the posts and see what information you can come across that people openly share about being an empty nester. The great thing about this is that the information you come across is organic. One downside to asking a friend is that they could reach on something they're not really struggling with just to give you an answer. The thing about pain points is that it's ongoing. You should set aside a little bit of time every month after your initial research to search through groups and continue to look for new pain points. The thing is pain points can evolve or change as time goes on, so it's important to keep a pulse on the market. Now that we've covered niches in depth, it's time to move to the next step.

Answering the Age Old Question: So What Do You Do?

If there's a common question that will come up again and again in your life it's, "So what do you do?" You're going to get asked this question when you meet new people, and you're going to be asked this question once you change careers into becoming a professional organizer. You might think it's such a simple question that it doesn't really matter how you answer it. You can just say you're a professional organizer and leave it at that. But that couldn't be further from the truth. When someone asks you this question, they're presenting you with an opportunity. It's an opportunity to generate a new customer, but in order to give yourself the best shot at this, you have to be able to answer the question in a way that's exciting and in a way that's not confusing. If you don't prepare for it, then being asked this question can throw you off. Sure you'll be able to give an answer, but it won't be as effective as it could be if you give it some thought. So let's go over how you can best answer this question.

Don't Hold Back

The first point I want to mention is that you shouldn't hold yourself back. What I mean by this is let's say you're still working a 9-5 job somewhere. You're going to start your organizing business on the side with the goal being to eventually do it full time. When someone asks you what you do, it serves you no purpose to mention your 9-5 job for what you do for your line of work. Sure, depending on what your job is and who's asking it may be appropriate. Generally speaking though, what do you stand to gain from mentioning your 9-5 job? Nothing! It's not as if you're going to get a pay raise because you brought in another customer for the business or whatever else the case is. This is something that I struggled with myself for years. When people asked me what I did, I would shy away from it. Since I was doing this business on the side initially I would talk about my day job. This felt comfortable to me. It wasn't going to raise any eyebrows or anything like that. I always had this fear that people would laugh at me behind my back and think that this business of mine was a joke. But you'll never know everything that's said about you and you can't control it anyways, so you might as well go for it! You might as well talk about your business when you have the opportunity because this can lead to a new customer, so you have nothing to lose and quite a bit to gain. But you don't just want to answer this question by saying that you're a professional organizer, you can do so much better than that.

So How Should You Answer This Question

You want to answer this question in a way that gets people interested so they'll continue to ask you more questions. The more questions someone asks about your business, the more the topic will stay on your business, which will help to warm up this new lead that you're creating. So you want to go for something that is more than just the basic, "I'm a professional organizer." You actually want to involve your niche as part of your answer. So here's one example of what this could look like:

"I help people who just became empty nesters reutilize their children's bedrooms."

Or

"I help busy moms organize their children's bedrooms in a way that gets the kids excited."

By saying a statement like this, you'll instantly catch people's attention. And if you're talking to someone who is in your niche, they'll become interested and want to learn more. Even if they aren't in your target niche, this statement can still create intrigue for someone to want to learn more, and now they have the chance of sharing your business to their friends. But can you see how when you set up your statement like this, it can't help but to draw people in? The cool thing is that you can take things one step further if you want to. After the first part of the statement, you can follow it up by saying without experiencing "blank" problem. This is where your research comes into play. If you've done your homework, then you know what some of the pain points are for your given niche. You can talk about that in your statement to take things up a notch.

"I help people who just became empty nesters reutilize their children's bedrooms without feeling like their violating a space that's not theirs."

Or

"I help busy moms organize their children's bedrooms in a way that gets them excited without any temper tantrums."

By saying this you're helping to create even more interest because people will want to know how you're able to do what you do. So whatever your niche is, think about how you can create a statement similar to what I've shared so that way you're ready when people ask you this age-old question.

You Need to Make a Plan

The next item on the agenda list is to create a business plan. This is going to be a short document that will only be about 2-3 pages long, but it will tell you how you're going to be operating your business. It's something you can refer back to as needed and it will give you a plan that you can execute on. Most people who are new to business skip this step entirely and that's a mistake. If you don't know what your business stands for, then you'll make poor business decisions that don't align with your goals. If you don't do a market analysis, then you can easily make a mistake with your pricing or how you market your company simply because of not taking the time to do proper research. Putting together a well-thought-out business plan will take time, but it is time well spent. This isn't something you want to sling together in half in hour. Take some time to do some research and think about the values that you want your company to have. The following should be included in your plan:

Company Overview

In this section of your business plan you're going to cover things such as how your company acquires customers, how does your company serve its customers, and who does your company serve. You want to think of this like a basic who, what, and why of your company and the customers that you want to have as part of your business. So if you've already taken care of deciding upon your niche, then this section shouldn't require too much additional thinking on your end. The marketing aspect will be covered in a later chapter, so you can fill in the details on that later. All that's left is how your company serves its clients. Think about this from a benefits perspective. What does someone gain by using your service? These are the things you'll want to include when answering this question. This can be things like less stress, peace of mind, being able to find things easier, better clarity, etc. The idea is to briefly cover these things as some of them will be covered more in depth later on.

Your Mission Statement

When you think about the military they have a goal that they're setting out to achieve. Failure on a mission isn't an option as it can have serious consequences. You want to approach your mission statement with the same type of belief. Print off your mission statement and post it somewhere that you'll see it on a regular basis. Remind yourself of it regularly as it will help to set the tone at the start of each day for you. Here's an example of a mission statement:

"At Sally Gets You Organized our mission is to provide the best service possible to our customers from start to finish. This means that from the time you first reach out to us even past when the project is complete, we will provide the best experience that we possibly can and will not stop until our customers are 100% satisfied."

Target Market

This is where you'll go more in-depth on who it is that you want to serve. So you'll want to include why you're choosing the target market that you are and why you believe you can serve this sector of people better than anyone else in your area. You also want to do an in-depth analysis as to who this person is. You'll create a character so to speak. So if your target market is busy moms in there 30s and 40s, what are some things they like to do when they're not busy with work or their family? What type of behaviors or characteristics do they have? By creating a client profile, you'll be better able to understand the needs and desires of your target market. For instance, if you're targeting a busy mom who has 3 kids and a full time job, you know she's probably putting her kids and her work ahead of herself. A lot of her needs are being neglected. So when you're creating marketing materials, you can speak to these things to help better resonate with them. So for instance, you could talk about how there's not enough time to get organized and even when you do clean, the kids mess it all up in less than a day. You can come in and help create systems to ensure that things will stay organized even if there are multiple children in the household.

Marketing Plan

In this section, you're going to go more in depth with each strategy that you plan to implement to gain new clients. So if one of your strategies is to use social media, then you'll want to talk about the type of content that you're going to post, how often you're going to post, what time of day you want to post, etc. You'll want to do this for each strategy so that all that's left to do is execute.

What Packages or Services Will You Offer?

You want to go over the different offerings that a customer could buy. For instance, are you going to offer virtual sessions, in-person, or both? Can someone buy an individual session or is there a minimum? How long will each session last for, etc.

Funding

How much capital are you going to need to start this business? You're not going to know in the beginning, but you'll want to take your best guess. How will you acquire the money necessary to start the business? Do you have savings? Will you borrow from friends and family or take out a loan? What are some of the ongoing expenses that your business is going to incur? Thinking about expenses before you start your business isn't very exciting and it's why so many people skip over it. However, if you skip this section then there will be expenses that come up that you're not expecting or are more expensive than you realized. Being successful in business comes down to generating revenue, yes, but that doesn't matter if you're unable to keep your expenses low.

Competitor Analysis

The last but not least section of your plan is going to be the aspect where you do a deep dive on your competitors. Why does this matter? Shouldn't you just focus on yourself? Yes, naturally that does make sense, but you need to figure out how you stack up against the competition so that you can properly outshine them. For instance, are all of the organizers in your area just generalists with no one specializing in a specific niche? What if someone is in the same niche you are? How many reviews do your competitors have? What kind of marketing strategies are they implementing? What are they charging? By knowing these things you can plan your business accordingly. Let's say someone in your area has a lot of reviews. Why should someone choose you over them? You're not going to be able to compete with reviews right off the bat, so you're going to need to figure out something else. This could be leaning on a competitive price point or leaning heavily on your niche with your marketing if this company doesn't have a niche.

Chapter 3: Tips When You're Organizing Spaces

We still have a lot left to cover in this book, but congratulations on making it this far! I know what's been talked about so far hasn't been the most fun things when it comes to business, but being boring is okay in business. So if you're someone who will take the information from the previous two chapters seriously, then I know you'll be able to do the same for the rest of the book. Don't skip around and cut out what you think isn't important. Sure you can modify things to suit your specific needs, but don't skip on writing a business plan because you don't think it makes a difference. Every detail in a business matters in order for it to be successful. One aspect of seeing success in this industry doesn't just have to deal with the business side of things, but the actual art of organizing spaces. Your skills for this may already be stellar in which case I applaud you! You might want to learn more or you might need to learn more before you feel comfortable taking on paying clients. Understand that each professional organizer will have their own way of going about things. So don't take the advice I'm going to share as the end all be all. Adjust and modify it as needed for your situation. So in this chapter, I'm going to share the things that I've found to work well for me. By being a better organizer, you'll be able to better serve your clients. This will result in better reviews and more referrals. You can be the best there is at generating new leads, but that skill will ultimately fall flat if you're unable to provide a high-quality service.

Create a Blueprint

One of the first things you're going to do before anything else is to create a blueprint. It can be tempting to want to dive in and start sorting through things and getting rid of the clutter. However, when a house is being built, the builders don't just jump right in. A blueprint is created first. There's a plan for the layout before anything else starts happening. This gives the builders something to work off of, a template to follow so to speak. You need to do the same thing with your clients. If you're working on a bedroom, for example, you need to draw out a blueprint that will detail how many square feet the room is. How long each wall is. How big the closet is. The dimensions of the bed. The dimensions of the desk. How big the dresser is. Doing this will allow you to know how much room you have. You'll know where the best place to fit each of the common bedroom items will be to fully optimize the space. If you're adding new items to the room, you'll be able to know if they'll fit and where they'll fit without having to guess. You'll be able to work off of your blueprint time and time again throughout the project.

Tips When Helping a Client Declutter

Here are some things you should think about when you are helping a client declutter their space:

Work in 3-4 Hour Time Blocks with 10 Minute Breaks Every Hour

The first tip that I want to share with you is an overall framework for how you should operate. It may seem like it's easy enough to continue to power through things in the beginning or that it's better to truck forward to get through the project, but you have to consider that you're human and so is the client. Do you put forth your best work when you're tired? We all do better once we have some little breaks here and there, and that goes for the client as well since they're going through this process with you. Therefore, it might seem wise to schedule a session for 6 or 8 hours if that's how long a typical workday is going to be anyways. This would be a mistake because the tail-end hours are not going to be nearly as productive as the hours at the start of the session. That's because by the end of the session, decision fatigue will have started to set in. This will make it harder to make sound decisions and you'll be wasting your time. Instead, you want every time you meet up to be productive and the way you ensure that happens is by scheduling in 3-4 hour time blocks. So if a space is going to take you 16 hours to complete, then that means it's going to take you 4 sessions, not 2 8-hour sessions. Because in reality, it's going to take you longer than 16 hours if you try and take care of everything across 2 sessions. The second thing you're going to want to do is take breaks. Again, this is not just for yourself but for the client as well. So be sure to take a 10-minute break every hour. This will help to keep everyone fresh throughout the session.

Don't Make a Client Get Rid of Something They Want to Keep

It can be easy in your eyes to say this or that item in someone else's home needs to go, but you're viewing things from an outside perspective. These items may have sentimental value to them. If someone is really struggling with clutter in their home, one possibility is that they struggle to let go of things. It's important that you let the client decide on what they'd like to get rid of and what they want to keep. You can of course give advice if they ask for it, but it's important to give people space to be able to make decisions. Some people will need more time than others to decide on what they want to keep and what they want to get rid of. If a client is struggling to let go of something, help them decide on where they can put it. Maybe it doesn't belong in the room it's in at all and can be better stored elsewhere in the home or stored offsite.

Don't Make Decisions on What to Get Rid of vs Keep Initially

Let's continue on with our bedroom example. If you have an extremely disorganized bedroom in front of you, it can be overwhelming when you're first starting. What you don't want to do is try and decide with the client what they want to get rid of vs keep. Instead, you'll want to start by doing the easy thing first. That's going to be throwing away trash or items that are damaged or broken. Why do you want to start the decluttering process this way? Well, the first reason is this will involve the least amount of brainpower. It's not going to take a lot of mental energy from you or the client. The decision is already made because it's obvious that it needs to be thrown away. It just hasn't happened for one reason or another. Secondly, this will give you a foundation to work from. When you do start going through items, you won't be sifting through trash that's in your way or trying to throw it away along the way distracting you from the task at hand. That will already be taken care of so you can focus more energy on making decisions. Thirdly, starting with the obvious gets the momentum going. Think about a workout. At the start of the workout, you might not be that into it. After a couple of exercises though, you're in a groove and it's easy to continue moving ahead. By starting with trash, it will make it easy to continue working and prime you for the harder parts of the session.

Place Items in Categories

After you cleaned up the room from any trash that's lying around, the next phase is going to be placing items in categories. Yes, it would seem to be faster and easier to just start going through items one by one and deciding if it should stay or go. This prep work will make that process far easier. There's no right or wrong way to go about placing items in categories. There just needs to be some basis for what you're doing. For example, if you were cleaning a toddler's room, you might create one pile for clothes, one pile for toys, one pile for books, and a pile for miscellaneous items. If you were organizing a bedroom that's shared by two siblings, then it would make more sense to have the clothing separate for each sibling, etc. So you can work with the client to determine what categories make the most sense or you can create your own categories based on what you're seeing in the room if that's what the client prefers.

Decide on What Belongs in the Room and What Doesn't

Once all of the items are placed in categories, go ahead and pat yourself on the back because you've done a lot of work just to get to this point! The next step in the process still is not to get rid of anything just yet. The reason why is that you can break things down a bit and doing this will make the decision-making process of staying vs going much easier. You're simply going to decide what belongs in the room vs what doesn't. You're not looking to get rid of anything at this point. This may seem like a lot of extra work but you have to understand how much harder it is to decide on keeping something versus letting go of it, compared to just leaving it in the room. After this phase of the process is complete, then the room itself will start to look a lot better and you haven't even had to get rid of anything yet! This wow factor will really impress the client and help motivate them to help them with what's about to come next.

Decide on What Stays and What Goes

The benefit of completing the process like this is that the room will be organized without making a single decision on having to get rid of anything. This means you can set out to do what you were hired to do and work around people who are struggling with getting rid of items. Additionally, by saving this step for last, the client will be able to see the progress they've made. They'll be able to see the changes in the designated area and this will help to inspire them now that the time has come to decide what needs to stay or go. The thing is by first deciding what stays in the room vs not first, this will help make it easier to see that the item isn't needed at all. Instead of it just sitting in a bedroom closet, why not get rid of it instead of having it sit in a different closet? Of course, some items will have sentimental value that people will want to keep. But the motivation combined with this realization, and combined with the upfront legwork that's already been done will make this process far easier than jumping right into it at the start of the project.

Tips for Staying Organized After the Project is Complete

Once you finish the job and leave, that is really only the beginning. As I'm sure you know, things that get cleaned and organized don't stay that way forever. In some cases, it doesn't take things very long for them to go back to the way they were. There are some things that you can do to help people stay organized past their initial project with you. Some of them will help to generate more revenue for your business, which is always a plus.

Do a Paid Follow-Up

One way that you can generate more income for your business is by doing a paid follow-up. You can come back to the client's home after a predetermined amount of time such as one, three, or six months later. During these sessions, you'll assess the current condition of the space that was organized, help to reorganize the space, and adjust any tips or advice as needed so the place can help to remain organized in the future. Even if you're not interested in doing a paid follow-up, you can still follow up with your clients for free after some time just to check in on them and see how they're maintaining things. This will go a long way for building positive relationships, it can lead to more business from your current client base, and it can help lead to referrals.

Something Comes in Something Else Goes

What's one of the biggest reasons why places that get organized tend to get disorganized as time goes on? It's because new things come in without any old items going away. Adding in one item doesn't seem like that big of a deal, and in fact, it is hardly even noticeable. However, as time goes on and on items will steadily start to come in one by one, and before you know it things have started to get out of hand. It's a lot harder for things to become disorganized if there aren't items to cause the clutter in the first place. Have the client implement a rule that if an item is to come in, then something else must go out. So if the client wants to buy a new shirt for example, then one of their old shirts must go. If they're buying some other item that will go in their room somewhere, then something else has to go. If this rule is followed, then it will help to naturally ensure that the room stays organized. This rule in and of itself might not keep things completely organized, but it will greatly help to reduce clutter. The problem with this tip is that it can be hard to follow. It's easy for someone to say, "Oh this won't take up that much space." Then next thing you know, things have gotten out of hand. You need to remind your clients of how their space looked before they started working with you and remind them that this is how clutter happens. It's just a little bit at a time and then things suddenly can look overwhelming. This is where you can come in and do follow-ups with your clients like I just mentioned in the previous tip. This will help give some accountability to your clients to implement what you're telling them to do because they know you're going to be checking in with them. One way you can approach this is by including at least one follow-up session as part of your initial package that you sell them so that it's built-in.

Label Storage Containers

Another little hack is to put a label on any type of storage container that you can. So if you're organizing a pantry for instance, then you would want to label each container or area with the items that belong in that section. So maybe your labels would be spices, cereal, pasta, snacks, etc. By doing things in this manner, you'll help to better ensure that snacks aren't put with the pasta for example. Instead, this will increase the chances that things actually go where they belong. The reason this works so well is because with a label, it will make someone feel inconsistent to put something other than pasta in a spot that's labeled for pasta. By doing this for any space that you organize, you can better help to ensure that things go where they need to, which in turn will help to keep a space organized.

5-Minute Pickup

The thing that makes clutter so dangerous is that it doesn't happen all at once. If it did, then it would bother us to immediately see a space go from pristine to a complete mess, so we'd do something about it. Instead, this clutter steadily increases as time goes on. Soon enough the clutter is overwhelming and yet it just stays there. Why is this the case? Well, it's because it's going to take too much effort to clean everything up and instead it's easier if it just remains. But who's to say you can't handle getting rid of the clutter the same way that it crept into your life? Why not get rid of it in small chunks at a time? The tip you can give to your clients is to have them set a 5-minute timer and only pick up during that time. There are a couple of things you have to do to make this effective though. Oftentimes people will lie to themselves and say that 5 minutes won't do any good, so they'll do nothing at all and wait for when they feel like doing more. The problem is that those feelings rarely come around. So it has to be a small enough barrier to entry to where the process doesn't require a lot of energy, hence the 5 minutes. Once the 5 minutes is up, then the person isn't required to do any more tidying up, they can stop if they want to. However, in a lot of cases, all you needed to do was get some momentum going and you'll want to continue the process. Really the 5 minutes is to just get things going and then a lot of times people will continue to clean.

How to Handle Difficult Clients

All of these tips and advice sound good in theory, but after you work with enough people you'll soon enough run into some difficult clients. In an ideal world, you'd be able to run through your process every time without a hitch, but that isn't going to happen. You are going to work with people who are going to pose a challenge to you. Some people may question your process, your expertise, or the reasoning behind what you're doing. Others may resist what you're trying to do or be plain rude. Some people will have good intentions but they'll overthink and doubt every little detail, which can make it hard to move forward. Sure some things you'll just have to live and learn as you gain experience. But what you can also do is learn so that way you'll know ahead of time how to work with certain people who can be a bit more of a challenge than a typical customer.

The Client Who Struggles to Let Things Go

It's easy to understand that you're going to come across people who have a hard time getting rid of items. To you or me, it may be obvious that their main problem with clutter has to do with owning too many things and that many of the things they have aren't serving them, but we're not in their shoes. So like I mentioned earlier, you have to be willing to meet them where they're at. You can only do the best you can with what they're allowing you to do. So they can't argue with the end result if they don't want to get rid of anything. Even though this is true, there are still some things that you can suggest such as offsite storage or storing items in an outside shed or different part of the home that can help with making the home less cluttered. Lastly, you can also follow up with them to see if they changed their mind about 6 months after you've worked with them. This can be a good way to continue working with them and bring in more revenue.

Remind the Client of Why They Hired You in the First Place

If someone is being stubborn and they continue to act like they know better than you, they put you down, or anything along those lines, you're going to need to politely challenge them. If you don't call out the behavior in one way or another, they're going to continue to run all over you and if you think about it, what good does that do anyone? If they know what they want and how to go about doing it, then why did they need to hire you or sign up for a consultation in the first place? So if you're working with a client like this, it can be helpful to ask them why they hired you in the first place. What were they looking to achieve by hiring you? To be completely honest some people like to be controlling or they want to feel knowledgeable, respectable, and powerful in front of someone who is an expert. Them hiring you might not have anything to do with organizing but instead control. With this type of clientele the best way to approach it is to get to the why. Oftentimes they'll say something along the lines of they hired you because they need help organizing. This opens the door for you to be honest with them. You could follow up with something like, "Thank you yes I agree, however, recently you've been combating every idea or suggestion I make. We are a team working together to achieve a goal, but it's difficult to do that when everything I suggest immediately gets swatted down. Do you think we can make this a collaborative effort?"

Handling Rude Behavior

Another difficult type of client behavior is when someone is being just plain rude to you. In most cases, once you call someone out on their behavior, they will stop. If you bring up an issue you're having with someone and it continues at this point you have a choice. You can continue to work with them, do what you can to get through the project and leave it at that, or you can let them go. Letting them go on your own terms can be difficult to do because it means you're going to be missing out on any remaining revenue from sessions you haven't completed yet. It can be hard to let go of the money that you worked so hard to earn in the first place, so either decision is understandable. The good news though is this type of behavior will likely show itself before they sign up to work with you. It can show up when you're emailing or messaging the potential customer, and it can of course show up during the initial consultation. When it happens before you've even officially signed them up, you have an opportunity to lay down some ground rules before they become a paying client. If the behavior doesn't show up until after they've started paying you, then you're going to need to politely call out the behavior. You don't want to get emotional or stoop down to someone else's level of behavior. Doing so can hurt your reputation and it will make it less likely that you'll actually get through to the person you're currently working with. The idea of calling someone out may be hard even if your approach and intentions are respectful, but you have to imagine the consequences if you don't. They will continue on with their behavior whether they intend it or not. You have to make them aware of how it's making it a challenge for you to work with them so that the goal can be accomplished. When you tie things back to the why, it makes it easier for the client to see how their behavior isn't being productive for what they hired you to do in the first place.

Do the Best You Can With What You've Got

If someone is being stubborn with where they want things to go or what they want to get rid of, then you just have to be willing to accept that things aren't going to look perfect with every client and that's okay. They're the paying client at the end of the day, so if they're happy, then that's what matters most. Sure, maybe the end result won't look good enough for you to post on your social media accounts, but that's okay. When you remind yourself of this mentality, it can help you overcome some of the frustrations that can come with working with a challenging client.

Chapter 4: How to Determine Your Rates as a Professional Organizer

Let's talk about money. Figuring out how much you want to charge for your services is a very important step in the process. Sadly, most people don't take the time to carefully consider what their service is worth and what others in the market are charging. As a result of this, newcomers tend to undercharge in the beginning. They'll look back on the time when their business started with regret because they know they could have made a lot more money than they did. I don't want you to have to worry about having that feeling, and fortunately, you won't have to. This chapter is going to cover some of the various ways you can go about charging for your service and help to provide some boundaries for what you should actually be charging.

What Type of Service Will You Offer?

The first thing you need to determine is the type of service you're going to offer. Will you offer only in-person sessions? Virtual sessions? Or a mix of both? You could offer only your initial session as a virtual session and then the rest can be in person. Or you could do purely virtual sessions. This will allow you to expand your reach as you'll be able to work with anyone, but it can be harder to achieve the same level of results as in-person and you'll charge less for virtual than in-person. Typically, it doesn't hurt anything to offer both virtual and in-person sessions. Why not have the best of both worlds? What will often happen is that you'll have people from all over see your social media pages and your website. So by offering virtual sessions, you'll be able to ensure that you're capturing leads no matter where they live. Then for the people that are in your area, you'll be able to maximize your revenue and your ability to serve them by offering in-person sessions.

Charge by the Hour, Session, or by the Project?

The next thing you need to decide is how you want to charge people. Realistically you have three options for how you can charge. You can charge people by the project, the session, or by the hour. Each option comes with its own set of pros and cons. So let's first start by talking about charging by the session. As I mentioned in Chapter 3, a good way to break things up is with a session that's 3 or 4 hours long, not 8 hours long. So if you're charging by the session, then you're essentially charging for 3-4 hours of your time and you're charging for that in one block of time. So you would essentially determine your hourly rate, multiply that by 3 or 4, and then charge that to your client. The benefit to charging by the session is you'll ensure that you're getting booked for a full session. You can also package up a certain number of sessions together to ensure that a certain project is going to get done. One downside though when doing this is how do you know how many sessions it's going to take in order to get the job done? You don't want to have additional sessions left over and try to find something else to work on, or worse yet, slow your working pace to eat up time. One thing you can do is have the client save the additional sessions for a later time, but this is something that some people simply aren't interested in doing. They'd rather have the extra money back. This is where the hourly rate can cover up some of the weaknesses that charging by the session may have. When you charge by the hour, you don't have to worry about finishing a project, and yet all of these extra sessions are still left unused. You don't have to worry about slowing down to eat up time. Instead, whenever the work is done, you can be done and charge them based on the number of hours that it took. This ensures that you're charging for the exact amount of work that's being done, which is a nice plus. There are downsides though. A client could cut things short at any point and leave a project hanging mid way through simply because they don't feel like paying you anymore. With the other options, you're going to be collecting more money upfront, which can help to protect you against this type of behavior. One way that you can combat against this though is to require a minimum number of hours. For example, someone wouldn't be able to book you for just one hour, they'd have to sign up for a minimum of 4 hours. Some clients can also be weary of the invoice. They might question the amount of hours that it actually took you to complete a project. Keep in mind, you're going to be billing them for your time outside of being with them. So if you're doing shopping for storage containers, that counts towards the billing hours. If they're messaging you asking questions, then this counts as well. Lastly, you can charge by the project, so if someone wants their kid's bedroom organized, you'll assess the situation during the initial consultation, talk with the client about what they're looking to achieve, and then you'll give them a price to complete the organization for that given space. The biggest downside to changing by project is that it can be hard to know how many sessions or hours it's going to take to complete a project. This means you could easily sell yourself short when you're giving out a quote. You might estimate that it will take 2 3-hour sessions to complete this project. In reality though it could take you 3 sessions and now you've just sold yourself short. The good thing though about charging by the project is that it's all upfront. The client knows what they're getting themselves into. So there's no questioning from the client for why they're getting charged for this or that. You can collect half upfront and the remaining half once the project is complete, or you can collect all of the money upfront, it's really up to you.

Which Method Makes the Most Sense for Your Business?

In the beginning, when you haven't worked with anyone yet, it can be hard to gain your footing to have that understanding of just how long it will take to complete things. You stand more of a chance of missing out on money and charging less than you should simply because a project can take longer than what you're expecting. For that reason alone, I would not recommend charging by the project when you're first starting out. As you gain more experience, charging by the project is something that you can give more serious consideration as it does have some good benefits to it. Starting out, you're going to be better off charging by the session or by the hour. If you decide to charge by the hour, then managing client expectations is going to be really important. You'll want to be transparent with them about what they'll be charged for and what they won't. Think about it from your own perspective. Do you like getting surprises on your phone bill or anything else for that matter? No one does! So, if your client is unaware that they're going to be billed for time when they're messaging you, they might not have asked the question in the first place. And as a quick side note, this can be a good way to cut back on the unnecessary questions from clients, so keep that in mind! Also be sure to send updates to your client for the amount of hours that they're at. During your initial consultation, give an estimate for how many hours you think a project will take and what you project the total cost to be. Of course, you'll also want to state it can go over this amount quite a bit as this is just an estimate. But by giving these regular updates, the client will know exactly where they stand, and it will give them the room to be able to cut a project short if they need to due to monetary constraints. Nothing will lead to a bad review faster than a misunderstanding with how someone is being charged or a client having a different expectation for what the cost will be than what it actually turned out to be. As long as the communication is good, then charging by the hour can be a good way to get started with this business. The other option you have is charging by the session. If you choose to go this route, I would give an estimate for how many sessions I think it will take to complete a project. If you're worried about suggesting 3 sessions when it's only going to take 2, for example, then cut things short one session from what you think it will take and then fill in the remaining time with an hourly rate. So if during your initial estimation, you think a project will take 3 sessions, tell the client 2 sessions and that you'll charge by the hour if additional work is needed to complete the project. Approaching things in this manner will ensure you're not overcharging the client. As time goes on, you'll get better with your estimations and you won't need to do this. The other way that you can approach charging by the session is to be upfront with the client about what you'll do with the remaining time if there is any. So let's say you give an estimate of 3 sessions. You could then say, "If this project only ends up taking us 2.5 sessions, what are some other areas of the house that you'd like to work on with the remaining time?" When you approach things in this manner, the client will follow your lead. They'll suggest to you another room or area instead of just asking for the remaining money to be refunded back to them. Even if they do suggest that, don't present it as an option. Just say that the estimation is as accurate as possible but you'd like to have a plan in place just in case there is extra time. All-in-all as you can see, there really is no one best option for everyone and it will all depend on what you feel the most comfortable with. For most people starting out, charging by the session is a good choice. If you don't mind being upfront with your customers, then charging by the hour is great as well. With this information though, my hope is that you'll be able to make the choice that's right for your business. And the beautiful thing about business is that you can always switch it up later on if it isn't working for you. So don't stress over it too much, pick something and just know you can pivot later on if you have to.

Create Package Promotions

If you are charging by the hour or by the session, one thing you can do is create package promotions. This is a good idea to help market your services in a fun and unique way. The idea behind this is to create a fun package or promotional offer that will help to book your appointments during times when you are slow. So for instance, if you want to work more hours during the day, but most of your clients work with you in the evenings, then you would create a package promotion but it can only be used during a certain time, such as a weekday from 10am-2pm, or whatever timeframe you want to work during. Or you could set it to where the package can only be used during a certain day of the week, such as Wednesday if that day is usually slow and you want more bookings. The next key to making a package promotion a success is to offer a discount from your normal rate. It doesn't do you any good if you charge the same rate, or else people will still continue to book during your most popular times. You need to incentivize people by offering a slight discount from your normal rates. So if for instance, you normally charge $75 an hour, then you could charge $60 or even $50 per hour. You want to come up with a fun name for your package as well. If you don't come up with a fun name, then it's going to come across as plain and uninspiring and your package won't do well. It's a good idea to come up with a name based on the time of year, the day of the week, or if there's a specific holiday that's coming up. So for example you could name your package Tidy-Up Tuesday, Tune-Up Thursday, or Spring into Action. Once you've come up with a unique name all you really need to do is finish setting up any additional parameters, and then you're ready to market your package. So for instance, not only do you want to control the day and timeframe that the sessions can be used, but you'll want to include a minimum number of hours or sessions. So for instance, the package may include a minimum of 9 hours or a minimum of 3 sessions. This will ensure that the package is worth your time. The customer is receiving a discount after all so it's only fair if you increase the minimum amount of time that someone has to work with you. Doing this will also give you even more consistency during your slow times.

How Much Should You Charge as a Professional Organizer?

Here comes the fun part, how much should you be charging as a professional organizer? Well, there's no one-size-fits-all answer to this question. There are a lot of factors that will ultimately determine what you should be charging as a professional organizer as opposed to someone else. Your location is a big one. You might live in a city and that would warrant you charging more than someone who lives in a more rural area. Even if you live in a city, there is a ton of variance between how expensive some cities can be compared to others. You also have your own level of experience and expertise. If you've been in business longer, then you should charge more than someone who is just starting out. So you have to be able to do your own research for professional organizers in your area and see what they're charging. See how many reviews they have to get a gauge on their level of experience and judge from that to determine exactly what your rate should be. Don't worry though, I'm not going to leave you hanging, I'm still going to give you a range for what you should be charging, but you'll need to think about the factors I just mentioned so that you can best determine where you'll fall within this range. With that being said, you should be charging somewhere around $50-$200 per hour. I know at first glance this can seem like a big range, but think about it. If you're someone who lives in Seattle and you have 5 years of experience, you should be charging closer to the $200 per hour mark. If you're just starting out and you live in rural Montana, then something closer to the $50 per hour mark is going to make more sense for you. If you were just starting out living in Seattle, then something in the realm of $75-$100 per hour would be a good place to start. Chances are good that you're not going to know exactly what you should be charging, but you can give yourself a good idea if you do market research and you consider the factors I just mentioned. The beautiful thing about pricing is that it's not permanent. If you decide you need to change things, then you absolutely can. You can lower your prices if you're generating leads but failing to close people. If your demand is through the roof and you can't keep up, then you should probably go ahead and increase your prices.

Once You've Determined Your Hourly Rate, Apply it to Everything

The good news is that once you determine what your hourly rate should be, you can now apply that to the other methods for how you want to charge. For example, let's say you want to charge by the session. If each of your sessions are 3 hours long, then you take your hourly rate, multiply it by 3, and now you know how much you should be charging per session. When it comes to charging by the project, you have to take an educated guess as to how many hours you think the project will take. Let's say you guess that a project will take you 9 hours to complete. Go ahead and take the number and pad it a little bit just to account for the fact that things usually take longer than you expect, so now we'll have 12 hours. You'd take the 12 hours and once again multiply it by your hourly rate to get the amount that you should be charging the customer.

Chapter 5: Considerations for Your Agreement Form

A good business practice is to use an agreement form before you start working with any client. It's a document that you'll have them sign and it will go over some various practices and policies that you'll want the client to agree to before you start working with them. In this chapter, I'm going to cover some of the things you should think about including in your agreement form. Right off the bat though, understand that this isn't something you just want to sling together yourself. It's best practice to hire an attorney to draft up this document for you. I do understand that this can be a bit of a pricey endeavor, but this is a one-time expense that you'll have with you for the rest of the duration of your business so keep that in mind.

Deposit

It's a good idea to collect a deposit from people who show interest in your business. Of course, this all depends on how you want to go about collecting the money. Are you going the payment in full route before you start working with someone? Are you going to collect half upfront and the rest once the project is complete? Are you going to send an invoice once the job is done and collect payment afterwards? There are pros and cons to doing each of the things I've just listed, but in most cases it's going to make the most sense to collect the money upfront. This will make your clients more committed since they've already paid and it gives you more leverage. A client can't suddenly drop you out of nowhere because they don't want to pay you. Of course, you can't charge upfront if you're charging by the hour, so keep that in mind. Let's think about a different scenario. Let's say someone is interested in working with you, just not right now. They want to start working with you a month down the road. What should you do in this scenario? Well, it would be bad business practice to just take them on their word for it. What will happen is they'll forget about it or lose interest in the idea and just move on never to be heard from again. That ends up being a hot lead that you missed out on. Instead, go ahead and collect a deposit from them, so that you're getting some revenue from the person. Now the person is also invested which is going to make them more likely to follow through with the service. From your perspective and the client's, there's another reason why you want to do this. Tell them that they have to put down a deposit to hold their place. You see, you only have so much availability on your calendar and it isn't fair to others who are willing to pay for someone else to hold a spot for free. So paying a deposit will allow someone to hold a spot on your calendar. Lastly, you have to think about what you want your deposit to be and if you'll allow refunds. Typically, I would charge a 25% deposit for the estimated scope of work and the deposit would be nonrefundable. What good does it do you for someone to eat space on your calendar just to ask for a refund at the last second? Those are appointments you could have had with serious customers, so not allowing for a refund can help to protect your business.

Sick or Unforeseen Circumstances

Have you thought about what you would do if you have a scheduled meeting with a client, but you're suddenly unable to make it? Well the obvious answer is that you would reschedule for a different time, and most of the time this will work out well no problem. But you do want to protect yourself in case the customer isn't being so cooperative. For example, let's say you have a session planned and it's right around the holidays. The client wants to get their home in order before all of their family comes over. You end of getting sick and you're unable to meet the deadline and the client is upset. The client isn't interested in rescheduling because the session will occur after the holidays which defeats the purpose of why they signed up in the first place. At this point, the client wants to cancel the session and get a refund. Yes, this is a really difficult scenario to imagine, but you have to prepare for these things to happen in your business. By having this policy in your agreement form, the customer will agree to being able to reschedule a session if you're unable to make it for whatever reason. By having this in place, you'll have something that you can go back to and remind the client of what they agreed to and why you won't be able to offer a refund. Sure in an ideal world, you'd be able to make every appointment every time without exception. And you are a professional so you will be on time 99% of the time. However, you might have car troubles, a family emergency, or a whole host of other things that could prevent you from being able to make it on time so it's best to plan for these things.

Cancellation/Reschedule Fee

Here's another scenario you need to think about, what if a customer contacts you and they need to reschedule? Just like in your case, life is crazy and unpredictable, but things are a little bit different. This is time that's booked on your calendar, so if someone reschedules at the last minute, then a spot was eaten up on your calendar for nothing. This is why you need to think about this and have a policy in place to help protect yourself. You need to think about how much of a notice you want in order for someone to be able to reschedule with you. In most cases this is going to be at least a 24 hour notice. If the customer needs to reschedule, then a fee will be charged, such as $25. Doing this can help to cut back on flimsy reschedulings or cancellations that just occur on a whim because it's not that convenient for the customer.

Reimbursements

Another aspect of this business involves buying items that relate to getting organized such as containers, labels, and other such items. How do you go about getting these items for the client? You do have a few ways you can approach this. You'll come up with a list of items that need to be bought, and the client can purchase them, or you can purchase them and be reimbursed for them later. If you are buying for the client, make sure that they approve what you're buying and the total amount before you do it. The problem with having the client buy the items themselves is that this can cause a delay in the process. It's easiest to do this when all of the items you're buying are online, and it soon becomes less practical if you're buying some items that are in a store. The good news is that you at least don't have to worry about getting refunded. In the other case, it is most often going to be easier for you to buy the items yourself and get refunded. You'll want to have something in your agreement form about getting refunded in case the client suddenly gets weird about not wanting to refund you for the items that you bought.

Travel Fees

You need to think about how far out you're willing to drive to work with a customer. This is completely up to you and the good news is that you can charge a travel fee which can help to offset some of the costs that you'll incur as a result of a customer living too far away from you. Doing this will allow you to expand your base of customers that you could potentially serve, so it does you no harm and can only benefit you. The way I would approach this is to not include a travel fee for customers that live within a certain radius from you, such as a 15-mile radius. Then you can charge a travel fee for each additional mile that someone lives outside of that radius. I recommend charging the standard rate given by the IRS, which at the time of writing is 65.5 cents per mile. So if someone lives 30 miles away from you, then you would charge a travel fee for 15 miles, which comes out to about $9.83. So to the customer this isn't going to be a big deal, but it's a big deal to you because you don't want your profit to be eaten into simply because you're having to spend more just to get to the customer in the first place. And if you really wanted to, you could charge a travel fee regardless of how far away the customer lives from you, but it's up to you on how you want to approach things.

When You Can and Can Not Be Contacted

By putting your available hours that you're allowed to be contacted in writing, you greatly increase the chances of your boundaries being followed and respected by your clients. This might feel a bit over the top, but it's important that you're able to establish hard times when you're not working so that you're able to avoid burnout. At any given moment, there's a long list of things that you could be doing, so you could always be working. You need to establish times when you will not be working and clients aren't allowed to reach out to you with questions. This is totally up to you and how you want to set up your schedule. I recommend taking at least one day completely off. So that could be Sunday for example, or you might want to have a day off during the week when you're less busy. You can also establish that you are not to be contacted after a certain time each day, such as after 8pm.

Refund Policy

It's important to have a refund policy in place so that the expectations are clear and you don't have someone requesting a refund when they shouldn't be. By having this rule in place you can help to avoid some of these situations in the first place. If something does come up, then you'll at least have the policy in place that you can refer to once the client signs the document so there's no discrepancy. You can keep your policy simple, such as once payment is made you will be unable to give a refund, or once the service has been rendered, a refund will not be offered. You of course want to do your best to accommodate to the client by rescheduling or doing what you can, but this is your business so you have to protect your income at all costs. Let's say someone signs up to work with you. They pay you, but they haven't used any of their sessions yet. They then tell you that they need to cancel because they're going to be moving and will be unable to complete the sessions. First off, you don't even know if this is true. People will most definitely make things up in an effort to get their money back. Secondly, it doesn't matter if someone is moving, you can explain this as a great opportunity to get a fresh start and offer virtual sessions as opposed to the in-person sessions. You can even mention specific accommodations such as doing virtual sessions as opposed to in person, if necessary, to help fulfill the service in an event such as this. The other main thing that you can do to help someone out is to reschedule, but what you don't want to do is hand out refunds left and right. That behavior will really hurt your business over time. Yes, sometimes you will run into tough situations, but as long as you prepare for them ahead of time, a lot of the hard part is already taken care of for you.

Unacceptable Client Behavior

This is something that a lot of people don't think about, but as I was talking about earlier sometimes you will work with some difficult people. You'll try the tactics that I mentioned, but still you're unable to get through to them and you're having a miserable time working with this person. Maybe they're being rude or demeaning towards you and the behavior simply isn't getting better. In these scenarios, it's best to move on from the relationship and focus on the clients that are respectful towards you. So you want to have a clause in your document stating something along the lines that you're allowed to terminate the working relationship between yourself and the client at any time when you deem the working relationship to be untenable. You'll also want to mention how a refund will be offered for the remaining unused sessions. This way things can kind of be left up to you for how you want to approach the situation instead of something specific having to happen before you can end things. By having something like this in place, you're once again setting up the expectations ahead of time so that the clients know what's expected of them and what can happen if you're rules aren't followed.

Chapter 6: How to Have a Successful Initial Consultation with Your Clients

Before you can transform a clients living space, you first have to assess their needs, goals, and the current situation. It can be hard to navigate your first meeting with someone but it's crucially important to make the most of your time so that the rest of the process is seamless. The last thing you want is to be backtracking and make it appear as if you don't know what you're doing because you don't have a good plan in place to follow.

Is Your Initial Consultation Free or for a Fee?

The first thing you need to decide is if you want your initial consultation to be free or if you're going to charge for it. If you go the free route, then your initial consultation is going to be part of your sales process. You're going to go through the assessment and then try to sell them to become a paying client. If you're charging for your initial consultation, then this means you've already sold the client and have begun working with them. Either way can work and there are pros and cons to each way of doing business. Let's first talk about the free route. If this is how you're doing things, then when you're emailing or messaging someone who's interested in your services, your goal is to get them to sign up for your free consultation. You don't want to go over pricing. If you give someone a price, they're going to judge your service based on that number without understanding the value behind it. Once they go through the consultation, they'll have a good understanding of the value you can provide, so once you give them your quote, it will make more sense and they'll be more likely to work with you. The benefit to doing this for free is that it will be easier to get people to sign up. Essentially it's like a free trial. You can show your value and the customer doesn't have to commit to anything. It lowers the barrier to entry, however this means you could be doing work for nothing if the person decides not to sign up. On the other side of things, your first session with a client could be after they've paid. If you go this route, you won't have to worry about working for free in a sense. Instead you'll try to sell a client either over email, messaging, or on the phone. Once they pay you, then the real work begins. However, it can be harder to get someone on board since they won't be able to experience the value you're able to provide in person. So which method should you follow? Well, I would say it comes down to your experience and sales ability. If you don't have any past sales experience, then this weakness could hurt you if you try and make your first session a paid one. By making your first session free, you'll be able to cover up your weaknesses and be able to play more to your strengths. Sure there's the risk of doing something for nothing, but it's something you'll have to tolerate as you gain more experience. Once you do gain that experience, then you can change the way you go about things. And of course, if you do have a good amount of experience, then you can skip straight to offering paid sessions only.

Will Your Consultation be Virtual or In-Person?

If you're truly looking to provide the best experience you can, you should offer in-person consultations. You may not be able to do this all of the time due to time constraints or simply because you have too many leads. In these cases, doing things virtually makes sense. It also makes sense to do virtual consultations if you're experienced and comfortable with your sales game and your organizational skills. Sure doing things in person will take more time, but it's for the benefit of you and the client.

Do Not Clean Up Prior To

Once you're talking to someone who is interested in your service and they sign up for a consultation, it's important that you tell them not to tidy up or clean before the consultation. This would be like working with a nutritionist who wants to see how you normally eat and you try to eat healthy to make yourself look good. The nutritionist can't see how you normally eat and therefore can't make improvements that fit within your schedule and lifestyle. Foods that you regularly eat and enjoy can't be implemented because you're trying to hide things. The same idea applies to getting someone organized. Their home or a certain room is the way it is for a reason. If they clean it up before you assess things, then it's going to make it really hard for you to implement things in a way that is sustainable. Things will quickly get out of hand soon after you stop working with them. So it's important to emphasize this point after they sign up for the consultation. If there are a few days in between when they signed up to when the appointment is, don't hesitate to remind them again closer to the time of their appointment. This will allow you to accurately assess the situation at hand.

Don't Try to Fix Anything

It's important for you to come into your first meeting with someone with the right expectations as well. The goal of the first conversation with someone is to assess the situation. You're not coming in trying to clean up or get rid of anything. You need to be able to first understand the situation so that you can develop a game plan that will best work for the client. Think about if you were to go and see a therapist. If the therapist immediately started giving you exercises to try and help improve your situation, you'd probably be confused. A good therapist will first listen and understand what's going on first before they try and give their advice or recommendations for how you can help improve what you're dealing with in your life.

How to Minimize Cancellations

One of the most frustrating aspects of your consultation is people canceling on you. This will happen 100%. It happens to everyone who is in sales. If someone tells you they've never had an appointment cancel on them, they are either lying or they've never had that many leads in the first place. If you're booking a lot of consultations, it will occur more often than you like. The first thing you have to understand is that it's going to happen no matter who you are or what industry you're in, so don't beat yourself up over it. In fact, it's not uncommon to have about half of your appointments cancel on you. This can vary of course depending on the quality of leads that you're dealing with. For instance, someone who just became aware of your business yesterday is more likely to flake as opposed to a friend you've known for 10 years. You're not going to deny someone simply because they've been following you for such a short period of time, so you just have to accept the possibility of it happening. So what are some things you can do to help minimize the amount of cancellations you get? The first one is a big one and it has to do with how far out their appointment is when you're scheduling them. You can manually schedule appointments when you're talking to prospects or you can send them a link to your calendar with available appointment times. Either way, you want to limit their options to make them pick a time that is sooner rather than later. You might be worried if none of the times will work for them, but simply let them know to tell you if none of the times work for them and you can figure something else out. Ideally, you want the appointment to occur within 24-48 hours from the time that you're booking the appointment. The sooner it can happen the better. It's always great if you could do the same day. Maybe you're talking to someone in the morning and you're able to go to their home in the evening. What you don't want is for them to book a week or two out in advance. Some people will be stubborn about this because in their eyes they don't see the harm in booking two weeks out. This however is a big problem for you because if they reached out, then they're excited about your business right now. A week or two later, chances are good those feelings have died down and this is where people cancel. People will also forget with it being that far out in advance and that's another barrier you have to overcome. Sometimes you won't be able to prevent this, but if someone is adamant that they aren't free until two weeks down the road, I'd suggest virtual as an option. You're more likely to see success that way. If they really want in-person, then don't worry, not all hope is lost. This brings me to my next point, which is to follow up, follow up, and follow up. It could make you feel like you're pestering people, but people are busy and they forget. You could book someone on a Monday for a Wednesday appointment and they could already forget about it. So you want to follow up 24 hours out, 12 hours out, and when you are on your way. If you have an appointment that's booked farther out in advance, then you'll want to send more reminders such as one every second or third day depending on how far away the appointment is. The further away the appointment is, the less frequent the reminders can be since you'll still end up sending more overall. For example, if someone booked two weeks out, I'd send email and text message reminders every three to five days until I get to the 24 hour mark. At this point I'd send one at 24 hours before, 12 hours before, and as I'm leaving. Sure this may seem like overkill, but you have to stay on top of people's minds or else they'll forget. Imagine if someone gives you no other choice and they book 3 weeks out. You have to make the most of it and remind them regularly. If you go three weeks and wait to communicate with them until the day before their appointment, what do you think is going to happen? They're going to cancel on you when you reach out! Regular follow-ups are key, and it's important to use multiple methods of reaching out to ensure that your messages are being seen. This is why it's a good idea to send a text and email, and possibly even a DM over social media to ensure they see it. When sending your reminder, you can make it super short and casual. You could send something like the following:

"Hey this is just a friendly reminder about your consultation appointment scheduled for May 27th at 6 pm. I'm looking forward to seeing you then!"

What If Someone Does Try to Cancel on You?

Let's say you reach out to remind someone of their appointment and they say they need to cancel. What should you do in this scenario? Well, you'd be leaving money on the table if you just left it at that. I'm not saying you should push them or question their reasoning for canceling. Instead what you should do is offer to reschedule for them. You want to make this easy on their part, so suggest some additional openings that you have available. Some people will take you up on this and others won't. Some will say that they'll reach back out to you when they're free and some people won't say anything about reaching back out. In either case, if you're unable to reschedule with someone when they cancel, then you'll want to follow back up with them. Typically, I'd wait about a week and then follow up to see if they have any free time to reschedule the appointment. Think about it, this person scheduled with you initially for a reason so they are interested to some degree. You don't want this lead to just die off without giving yourself a fair shot at closing the deal. You have nothing to lose by reaching out so you might as well do it as this can help to cut down on missed opportunities.

Questions to Ask to Make the Most of Your Time

The questions you ask someone as part of your initial meeting with them can really set you up for success or cause you to fail and have to backtrack. It's important that the client has the right expectations and asking the right questions will ensure that both parties are on the same page.

What is the Goal When it Comes to Getting Your Space Organized?

This is a great place to start because clearly there is a pain point that the customer is experiencing or else they wouldn't have reached out to you in the first place. That's really what you're trying to get to the heart of here. If you can determine what's wrong, all you have to do is fix that thing, and the customer should be happy. If you don't ask a question like this then it can be hard to define an outcome that you can achieve and say, "Hey, look at what we did." Asking for the goal is the first step, but there are follow-up questions you need to ask that pertain to this as well. For instance, does the client have a particular space in mind or is it the entire home that they want organized? If they're not sure or they say it depends on pricing, then go ahead and ask them which room bothers them the most. Then you can give quotes just for that area and for the whole home if you need to. The other question you want to ask here is whether the goal is to get rid of things or keep what they have but make it more organized. This question will give you a peek into what it will be like to work with this person. If they say they aren't looking to get rid of things, then you know you're going to have more of a challenge when it comes to organization. That's fine though as you can work around this, but it's better to know this information up front rather than to fight against it during your sessions.

If You Could Snap Your Fingers and This Space Would Look Perfect to You, What Would That Look Like?

Once you have the goal, the next thing you want to do is have the client start visualizing and painting a picture of how things would really look. If you're organizing an entire home, then they can go over key areas of their home such as children's bedrooms, the living room, kitchen, etc. This is an effective question not just for you, but for the client as well. It will help them to get excited and eager to start the process because they'll want to make their vision a reality as soon as possible. From your perspective, asking this will help to add more description to what their goal is. You'll have a much better understanding of what you need to do to make the client happy. If they say they just want to be able to open their pantry and easily spot the bread, then you know you need to make that happen when you're planning things out.

Why Do You Believe Your Home Has a Hard Time Staying Organized?

The answer to this question will help you determine a game plan for how the person or family can stay organized even after the job is done. For instance, maybe a lot of the cleaning falls on one of the parents and the kids don't help out too much. Well, now the parent is constantly working against everyone else in the home making a mess, which is a disaster waiting to happen. So you can help suggest things such as getting rid of something to bring something else in or doing a 5-minute pickup to stay on top of things. Or maybe the kids don't pick up because they don't have adequate storage to put their toys up, so now you know you need to focus on storage in order for the organization work that you do to be sustained.

Take Measurements of the Space You're Organizing

Once you ask your initial set of questions, you'll then want to start taking measurements. For example, how many square feet is the room? What's the length and width of shelf space in the closet? How big is their bed? How big is their desk? Are they willing to buy new furniture to make everything fit better, etc.

Create Your Blueprint

Now that you have your measurements, you're now ready to create your blueprint. The best way to do this is to start sketching out your blueprint as you're taking your measurements. It's easier too when you're in the actual room as opposed to having to remember little nuances that the room may contain.

Send them a Quote

Once you've completed all of your measurements, thank the person for their time and let them know you're going to put together a quote for the project. This quote is where you will really sell the person on your services. Obviously, you'll skip this step if you've already sold the person before the first meeting. But as part of this quote, you don't want to just include pricing, you want to spell out the whole vision for what you plan on doing. Lay out a step-by-step game plan. Include a visual mockup of what you plan for the space to look like once the project is complete. If all you include is pricing, it's going to make your quote look boring and it will be less successful. You want to create a PDF that looks visually appealing. Use your brand colors and logo. Imagine a document with fun colors as opposed to a plain document that has text on it. It won't convert as well that's for sure. So the way to layout your quote is to start by thanking the customer, then reiterate some of the things that were discussed, followed by the step-by-step plan you plan on using to reach the end goal, a visual drawing or presentation of what the end result will look like, and lastly the price to complete the project. All in all the total document shouldn't be more than 2 or 3 pages at the most. You also want to be sure to break up each section with headings and bullet points. You don't want everything to be one big block of text. It's important to list the price last because you want to build up the value from your offer first before they see the price. If they see the price before anything else, then there's a higher likelihood that they leave the document and you never hear from them again. You have to build up the value by putting the other things first and then come in with the price. If you're charging by the hour, list your price per hour, but you may be hesitant about putting the estimated number of hours. When you're new, it can be difficult to gauge how many hours a specific project will take. If you underestimate the number of hours, it may upset the client because they're paying more than what they thought even though you said it was an estimation. On the other hand, you could overestimate the amount of hours to ensure the project is completed in less time. The customer won't be upset about this as it will be saving them money. However, the overall price will look bloated so it can make them more hesitant to sign up in the first place.

Include a Link to be Taken to Checkout Page

Part of your quote has to include a link that will take the customer to a webpage where they can pay. You want to make things as seamless as possible to ensure that people are able to sign up for your services. You want to make sure the link actually works, so test it out yourself. What I recommend doing is creating a $1 invoice in your PDF, send it to yourself, and checkout as if you were a new customer. This way you'll be able to see if there are any hiccups throughout any step in the process. If the payment goes through, then you know you'll be good to go to collect payment from other people. If you don't test this, you run the risk of something not working and missing out on a potential sale. You've done so much hard work to get to this point, so this is the last thing that you would want to not have work. You don't want to assume that the customer will reach out to you either because some people will and others will simply not pay. Then you're reaching out asking what's going on and they tell you it's not working. It's just an embarrassing look on your part that can totally be prevented. As far as options are concerned for collecting payment, you have quite a few options. You can use something like PayPal, Stripe, Square, Wave Accounting, Google Pay, Apple Pay, and many others. It's not a bad idea to give people more methods to pay than fewer. So for instance, you'll definitely want people to have the option to pay via a credit or debit card, which you can set up using something like Stripe. But in addition to this, you can offer additional options such as PayPal or Apple Pay to make it more convenient for people who already have accounts set up and may prefer to pay using one of those methods.

How to Book More Consultations

In order to book more consultations, you first have to generate more leads. By marketing your business, you're making people aware that you exist. The first step in any business relationship is to make people aware that you even exist. After this, your goal is to continually expose these individuals to your content so that they can get to know you and your business better. The idea is that eventually they will sign up for your consultation and this allows you the opportunity to sell them to become a paying customer. The thing is that the majority of people who are aware of your business won't be interested in taking the next step. This doesn't mean you should give up on them, it just means they're not ready right now. Let me give you an example of this. I had a friend who started a pest control business and he reached out and asked me if I had any pest control issues at the moment. I thanked him for reaching out, but I said that I didn't. Three months later for whatever reason, I started getting a bunch of millipedes in my home, sometimes scooping up as many as 20 per day! So you bet this problem caused me to spring into action and reach out to him. So I suddenly went from someone who wasn't interested to a hot lead because my circumstances had changed. If he had never reached out, then I would have no idea he was doing pest control. So when I did become a hot lead, it would have been for someone else had he not made the effort that he did. So all of this is to say that the actions you take today may not have a noticeable impact on your business immediately. Instead, it might be 3,6, 12, 18 months, etc. down the road before someone finally decides to reach out for one reason or another. I can't tell you how many times someone has reached out and said, "I've been following you for a while now and I think I'm ready to make some changes." It's all of that past effort that's been put into marketing that snowballs and adds up to make a difference. So if you want to increase your revenue, you have to make more sales. To make more sales, you have to book more initial consultations. To book more consultations, you have to do more marketing. Luckily that's what the entire next chapter is dedicated to. As with everything else, it's an important part of the process so you'll want to pay extra close attention. Every other step in the process will crumble if you mess this up. Remember, you're only as strong as your weakest link, and this link in particular is a big one that you don't want to get wrong.

Chapter 7: How Do You Get Clients as a Professional Organizer

One of the biggest problems you're going to face as a new business owner is the fact that nobody knows who you are when you're starting out. When you think of some of the biggest brands in the world they continually pour millions into their marketing to constantly remind their customers of who they are. All though you may not have that kind of capital to invest in a marketing campaign, you still need to approach things with the same mentality. You must continually pursue the acquisition of new customers and continually remind people about your business. If not, you will soon fall to the wayside.

Social Proof is Really Important

When you go to buy something, how important are the reviews in helping you make your decision? My guess is that they definitely have an influence over you one way or the other. Positive reviews can influence us to buy not just because the feedback is good but because we want to be in with the crowd, so to speak. If everyone else is buying something, you may buy just because that's what everyone else is doing. Sadly, the opposite effect can occur. Bad reviews or no reviews can influence someone to not buy your product because we don't know if we can trust it. We have to invest our time and money into the products we buy so we can look to what others have to say to help shortchange the research process and build or destroy our trust with the product or service. The problem is a product could be amazing, but nobody is willing to try it out because of the lack of social proof. In your case, it's not going to be negative reviews that are going to hurt you, it's going to be the lack of reviews. So if you need social proof to get more clients, but you need clients in order to get social proof, what are you to do? The best way to overcome this issue is to leverage the people who do already know who you are. You already have people in your inner circle who trust you, so even without any reviews, they're going to be far more likely to take you up on an offer than a stranger. A stranger is going to need more social proof to take you up on your service. Sadly, ego gets in the way for a lot of people here. They themselves look to reviews when making purchases, but then try and downplay their importance when it comes to their own business. I don't want you to be like this. If you approach what I'm about to share with you with humility, then it will lead to your success sooner than later. What is that idea exactly? It's simple, you're going to leverage people who already know you by reaching out and asking if there are any organizing projects that they'd like for you to take on for free. Yes, that's right, for free. Most people don't like the idea of working for free, and I get it, but that thought process has to be set to the side. Think of this as an investment in your business that will continue to pay you for years and years to come. It's not as if you have to organize someone's entire home either. It can be something as simple as a pantry or a closet, or even just a room. So how should you go about this? Well, start with some of your closest friends and text them. Also message acquaintances on social media. Your goal is to get as many people as possible to take you up on the offer. Even though it's free, you're still going to need to message quite a few people. Ideally, you'd want to get at least 5 projects under your belt, but 10 would be ideal. Not only will these projects be a good way for you to gain social proof, but it will also allow you to practice for free without the pressure and expectation that comes with a paying client. Here's the message you can send to people:

"Hey Susie I hope you've been doing well! I recently started my own organizing business and I'm looking to take on some projects big or small for FREE to help get things going. Is this something you'd like to learn more about?"

People are busy, so you don't need to bombard them with a long text that they might not read. Your response rate should be pretty good depending on how well the person knows you, but expect a lot of people to not take you up on your offer. Once you do get someone to bite, be sure to let them know that you're going to use before and after pictures in exchange for doing the project for free. It's even better if you can also get a video testimonial of someone explaining what it was like working with you. Once you start getting your social proof, you can go ahead and put it on your website and start to post it on social media regularly. Yes, that's right, post and repost your social proof on social media on a regular basis! Post it on your feed, and post it on your story again, and again, and again! You have to. Your account is going to get new followers who will never see the social proof that gets buried on your feed. Even your current followers will forget if you post about it once and leave it at that. You have to constantly remind people other people are interested in what you do and their lives have changed for the better because of it.

Keep the Snowball Rolling

As you start to get more clients, you'll want to be sure to get their permission to use before and after pictures of the project you did for them. Again, coupling this with a video testimonial is even better. You'll want to do this for every client who you get paid or not because there is no such thing as too much social proof. There's another layer to this and that's with your online reviews, such as the ones on Google. These are very important as well for improving your search engine optimization and making it more likely that people will find and use your business when they are conducting online searches centered around professional organizers. So at the end of your last session when you're working with someone, ask them if they wouldn't mind leaving an online review for you. Most people will say yes, but remember follow-up is king here. People will have good intentions, but they'll forget or they won't do it because it's too much of a hassle to figure out on their own. Wait roughly 24 hours and if you still don't see a review, follow up with them via email and text. Ask them again for the online review and send a link that will take them straight to the page to leave a review. This is how you'll generate more online reviews because you're making the process simple. You're taking the guesswork out of the equation for the other person. Once you send that link, wait another 48 hours, and then follow up again if you haven't seen the review come through yet. Sometimes you do have to pester people a bit to get what you want, but you'll want to strike while the iron is hot. As time goes on and you have more reviews, you could be more lax about this, but stay on a hot pursuit with your first set of customers to get those reviews because they matter that much!

Create an Email Newsletter for Your Organizing Business

Email is far from dead even if things like messaging have increased in popularity over the years. The main benefit that an email newsletter will give you is that it will be another method for you to be able to stay in regular contact with your customers or people you are trying to convert into becoming a customer. There are plenty of different email newsletter providers out there. Some good ones are

AWeber, Constant Contact, and Mailchimp. Essentially what these services do is allow you to create an email and send that email to your entire list with ease. You can also segment your list. This means you could create an email and only send it to certain people. For example, if you had a new offer you were trying to promote, you could filter out people who have already clicked on your link so that you don't have to worry about annoying those people. The question is, how do you get people to sign up for your landing page? You can set up landing pages or a simple sign-up form on your website so that your potential customers' email addresses can be captured and added to your list. Once someone joins your list, you can set up a list of automated emails that will be sent to someone automatically after they sign up. As an example, you could set up a series of 5 different emails that will be sent to anyone who signs up for your list over a period of 10 days. You can set up your initial sequence to be as many emails as you like and they can be sent as frequently or infrequently as you like. Once someone goes through your initial sequence, then they'll just receive your regular newsletter updates. What are some things that make for an effective email campaign? A common mistake is to constantly use your email list as a way to send pitch after pitch or promotion after promotion. If you do this, it will make your audience numb. People will either ignore your emails or they'll unsubscribe. Instead, you need a more balanced approach between providing helpful information and then offering a promotion of some sort. You could use a ratio of 5 informative emails for every 1 promotional email that you want to send. What would your informational emails look like? This is a great opportunity for people on your email list to get to know you better. You could send an email where you list out 5 facts about yourself, one of which is false and then you could have people reply to the email and guess which fact they think is the false one. This is a great way to have your subscribers get to know you better and to get them used to replying to your emails. Other educational emails you send could be things such as tips for getting your home organized and keeping it organized. You can use a good mix of content that allows people to get to know you better and actual content relating to getting organized. Then when it comes to your promotional emails, you'll want to be sure to create urgency and provide a link that will take people directly to a sign-up page. For instance, let's say you're running a promotion to kick off the spring season. You want to include a reason why people should sign up now and not later. It's easy for people to push things off, forget about it, and then never come back to it. By creating a sense of urgency, you'll help to increase your sales. The way that you can create urgency is by limiting the time that the deal will be available and/or limiting the amount of people the deal will be available to. You could start the deal on a Monday and say the promotion will end Friday at midnight, so be sure to get in on the savings while you can. The other approach would be to tell people that you're only doing this for the first 5 people who sign up, then you're taking away the offer. You can combine both of these methods by saying that the deal will end on Friday at midnight or when 5 people sign up, whichever comes first. A common mistake people will make when they're doing promotions is they'll send one email and that's that. Well, people are soon going to forget about your offer. If you're starting a promotion on Monday and saying it ends on Friday, people aren't going to feel the urgency to take action. Instead what you should do is send people one email per day during this promotional period to continually remind them of the deal that's present. Then you would really need to ramp things up during the last 24 hours of the deal. This would mean emailing people at the 24, 12, and 1-hour marks before the deal ends. It might feel like you're pesting people, but this is when the urgency is going to be at its highest so you need to take advantage of it. After all, the whole point of your email list is to generate more sales for you. If someone unsubscribes because of getting too many emails, so what? You didn't miss out on anything because they probably weren't going to buy anyways.

Create Business Social Media Accounts

It's no surprise to you that your customers are on social media, so this is a great place to generate leads. It's not a huge deal for which platforms you're on because your target audience is likely going to be on any platform that you want to use. What matters more is that you focus on the style or personality of a particular platform. Focus more on the platforms that align with how you want to make content and what makes you feel the most comfortable. Once you're on social media, that in and of itself isn't enough to really make a difference. Everyone is on social media and it can be hard to separate yourself from the sea of other content that's out there. To be successful using social media as a business owner, you first and most importantly have to put your ego to the side. You're in the professional organizing business and as such the only thing you should care about is driving more sales. If you make a post that gets one like, but that one like is someone who becomes a customer, that post is more effective than a post that gets 120 likes but leads to 0 new customers. Also, you're in the organizing field. Yes, plenty of people will be interested in this field. Don't kid yourself though into thinking you have the potential to create as much interest as a page that's for pure entertainment. It isn't going to happen because people go on social media to keep up with their friends and be entertained. They're not going there to be sold to. That's a key thing you must understand. People are not going to social media to look to hire a professional organizer. You have to continually show up and convince people that they need your services. When you approach social media with this mentality, you will be much more successful. You'll understand that it takes more effort to gain a customer than someone else who's frustrated after making 2 posts and not gaining a customer from it. So don't get discouraged from a lack of engagement or from nothing seemingly coming from your posts. As you continue to post time and time again, you're steadily gaining the trust of your followers and before you know it, the leads will start to come in. This really should go without saying but you have to be consistent on social media in order for this to work. You need to decide how often you're going to post on social media, which could be 3 times per week to start out. You can always increase things from there, but you need to start out with something that you think you can maintain. As far as content is concerned, you want to follow a similar approach that you would with your email list. You want to provide value for about 5 or so posts without expecting anything in return, and then you want to come in with a promotion or offer of some sort. You don't want to continually spam out offers, but it would also be a mistake to never throw out some bait either, so to speak. When it comes to your regular content, what should you post about? The following are some ideas:

Client Testimonials

One of the biggest aspects of gaining new clients is going to be social proof. So any type of social proof that you gain, you want to be sure to post it and post it regularly. This can be on your feed or your story. You can get multiple forms of social proof from just one client, so this gives you some good content that you can repurpose. So for instance, get some before and after pictures, but also get a video testimonial, and now you have two different forms of proof from one client that you can post on your feed and then regularly post on your story. What you can do is regularly cycle through your testimonials and post them on a weekly basis. You constantly want to remind your followers that you're able to get great results for your clients.

Organizing Tips

You may think that you'd want to keep your best-known tips and secrets to yourself so you can share them with your paying clients. You certainly don't have to share everything with your followers, but you do want to share some advice that can actually help people out. Take something and break it down into smaller pieces so that you get more content out of it.

For example, if you were to share the 4 steps to getting a bedroom organized, break each step up into its own post. This will help to create excitement with your audience as well because they'll be following along waiting for the next tips.

How to Keep Your Home Organized

Getting your home organized is one thing, but keeping it that way is a whole different challenge. You can make content centered around giving advice for staying organized. Again the fear here is that people will take your free advice and run with it and they'll never hire you. That is a rational fear, but you have to remember people struggle to get and stay organized for a reason. Part of that reason is that they need outside help for one reason or another. It could be too overwhelming or they're not sure where to start. There's a certain level of accountability that someone is going to gain by hiring you and that's something a follower is never going to be able to gain by reading a social media post.

What's Going on in Your World

Don't be afraid to post things about your personal life either. People want to get to know you better and social media is the perfect way to be able to do so. Share what you're eating for dinner. Share a book you're currently reading or a podcast you're currently listening to. What kind of pets you have. It can be anything that you're willing to share, but this will help your audience get to know you better which in turn will help build more trust with your audience.

Be Vulnerable

It's hard to be vulnerable. It doesn't matter if it's in a relationship or on social media, it can be hard. But I want you to hear me out here. Social media can oftentimes be this place where we only post about the high moments in our life. We try to make it seem as if we have it all figured out. As a professional organizer, it would seem unprofessional if you posted a picture and caption about your home being unorganized, right? Or if you talked about the struggles of being a small business owner? Surely doing things like this would turn people away, right? Well, I'm here to argue that doing things like this will actually attract more people to you. People want to work with someone who is real and authentic. If you're able to share how even you struggle with keeping things organized 100% of the time, guess what? People are going to be able to relate to that. They're going to know that you're realistic in your approach to getting organized, that it's hard work no matter what, and that no one is perfect. If you have kids, then you can talk about the struggles that come with staying organized when you have little ones running around who really don't care about the home staying a certain way. Whatever it is, this is your platform and therefore your chance to stand apart from the crowd. I can almost guarantee that your competitors are not doing this and it's a great opportunity for you to be able to differentiate yourself. Yes, it is hard to make posts like this, but some of your most liked posts will be the ones where you open up about the struggles you're going through, whether it be in your business or personal life.

Get Referrals from Your Current Customer Base

Once you've worked with someone, you're missing out if you don't get their help to gain more clients. It's hard enough to get someone to trust you when they don't know you. But when a friend recommends a company to you, how likely are you to trust their recommendation? You're very likely to trust it because you know they don't have an incentive to lie to you and you trust their opinion. Once you've gained a customer, you want to do what you can to get them to recommend you to their friends. One way that you do this is by simply being so amazing that they can't help but to talk about you. The other way and what you'll more than likely have to do is incentivize people. People may or may not be interested in getting a discount the next time they use your service because there may not be a next time. What you can offer instead is to give them a partial reimbursement on their previous session if they refer a new customer to you within 30 days of using your service. You could offer a 15% reimbursement if they refer a friend who actually pays within 30 days. You don't want to give someone 15% back just for this person to not even sign up. The way you can use this effectively is to wait until after the job is complete. This way the person is feeling happy and excited because of what you've just been able to do for them. This is when they'll be the most likely to refer you to a friend.

Partner with Other Companies such as moving Companies or Restoration Companies

This might seem a little odd to you, but think about it. If you partner with another company, what you can essentially do is trade leads. For example, if you know of someone who would be interested in a service of a company you're partnered with, then you can refer the person to that company. In exchange, the other company will do the same thing for you, so it's a win-win. You have to go about doing this in a way that's productive though. You don't want to be partnering with just any company. It needs to be a company that would make sense to be used with your business. So something like a moving company, or a restoration or remodeling company would make sense. Once someone moves, they'll be more likely to want to get off to a fresh start and have their belongings get settled in a place that makes sense for them. The same premise applies for a restoration or remodeling company. Once someone gets their home remodeled, they will be more likely to want to have their things reorganized. What you need to do is reach out to these various types of companies in your area. You can email, call, or reach out via their website. Mention who you are and what you do. Talk about how you'd be more than happy to send any leads their way and ask if they could do the same for you in exchange. This will yield you some results but it will work better if you can toss a lead their way first. This will show that you're serious about the relationship and that your business is capable of building relationships that can benefit other companies. Once you do this, other companies will be more likely to send leads your way. Due to this, if you're unable to send leads, it can be hard to gain traction from this initially. However, once you get things going, you'll be surprised when leads start to trickle in from other places.

Collaborate With Other Professional Organizers

Along the same lines as the previous tactic, it's also a good idea to collaborate or partner with other professional organizers. At first glance, this may seem even more strange that you would want to collaborate with someone who's in the same field that you are, but hear me out here. The reason why you want to build relationships with other people in your space is twofold. The first is that you'll be able to learn from their experiences. This will allow you to learn from their mistakes and tweak how you do things because you're going to be learning directly from someone else who's doing the same thing you are. Secondly, you'll be able to give each other leads when appropriate. Photographers do this all of the time. They know of other photographers in the area and it's important that they build these relationships. Why you ask? Because let's say they get sick or have a family emergency arise on the day they're supposed to be shooting someone else's wedding. Obviously, the wedding date isn't going to change last minute, so someone else needs to step in and cover for them. In exchange, the photographer will cover for them if anything arises. By doing this, it allows both photographers to make more money and have opportunities that they wouldn't have otherwise had they not formed this connection. In the same way, you want to build relationships with other organizers in your area. They can step in for you in a pinch and you can give them less than what the overall job is worth so that you can still make something off the job. Another scenario could be that you get a lead that isn't a good fit for you. Maybe you don't think you'll mesh with their personality. Maybe the project is too big or maybe you have too much on your plate right now. You can toss the lead to someone else. If you just deny someone, they're going to go to your competitor anyways so you might as well be the one to refer them! Now what this does is it makes it more likely that another professional organizer will give you leads that they're unable to fulfill. For you to be successful with this, you have to change from a scarcity mindset to a mindset of abundance. It can be easy to think that there aren't enough leads in your area so you have to keep them to yourself even if you're unable to fulfill the service. The truth is there are plenty of leads for everyone, what is more likely to be the problem is either your ability to generate leads or close them. And pay attention to this yourself. You'll notice that when you're not worried about where your next client is going to come from, people will reach out to you more. When you stress and fixate on things, you tend to continue to get more of nothing. Staying in a scarcity mindset isn't going to serve you anyways so you might as well focus on abundance. When you focus on abundance you're not worried about some competitor stealing your lead. Instead, you know that when you share a lead with someone else, you will be repaid back even more in some way down the road.

Ultimately when it comes to generating leads for your business everyone always looks for the next big tactic or strategy and they think they're doing the wrong activities, and that's why they're struggling. You'll notice that I didn't list a ton of different methods here and that's because you don't need a ton of different strategies. What you do need is to instead focus on each strategy that you do with more intensity. For instance, most people will say that building connections doesn't work, but in reality, they only reached out to two other companies and said it doesn't work. What you have to do is continue to reach out more and more until it does work. If you focus less on what strategy you should do and instead put that energy into more effort for the strategy, you will be better off.

Conclusion

Building a business takes a lot of time and effort. There is no way around this fact. The good news is that you'll be doing something you're passionate about and that you'll enjoy. This passion will allow you to work longer and harder than you would for something that you don't care about. If you're working a 9-5 right now and you have a family, then you know that adding in a business on top of your other responsibilities is going to be extremely tough. There are going to be days when you doubt yourself. Days where you question if you should have ever started this business in the first place. Days where you feel like quitting and just accepting a normal life with a 9-5 job. I tell you this so you can mentally prepare yourself for what's to come. When these moments do come I want you to remember that you expected this and that you can overcome it. You can make it out to the other side. There's a reason why you wanted to become a professional organizer in the first place. You have to keep that reason strong in your mind when you start to doubt yourself. Understand that the tough times will fade away so long as you're able to withstand and outlast them. I don't say any of this to discourage you, but to instead be real with you because business is tough. By knowing this ahead of time, you'll be mentally prepared when things get hard. And you'll be ready to push through to make it to the other side. If you believe in yourself and don't quit, then how can you fail? Your dreams are bigger than your desire to give up!

www.ingramcontent.com/pod-product-compliance
Lightning Source LLC
Chambersburg PA
CBHW050103230526
45470CB00004B/1656